This 1868 drawing shows Old San Francisco in rather distorted perspective.
The Cliff House and Seal Rocks are in the left foreground. Proceeding through
the Golden Gate with its heavy ship traffic, one can see the Presidio, Marina

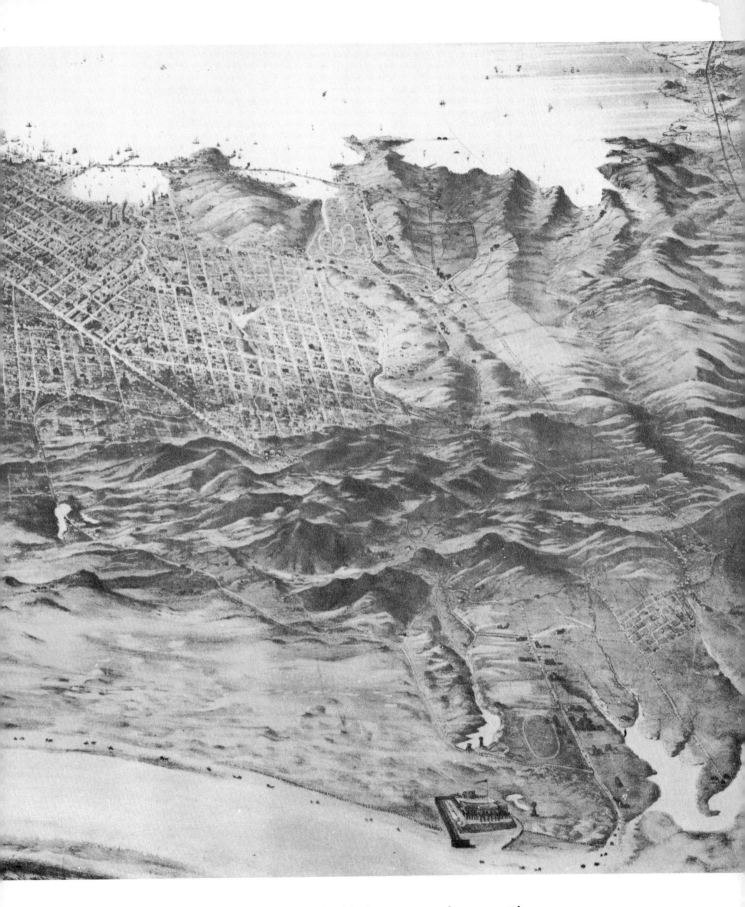

Green, Fort Mason and Fisherman's Wharf. Market street can be seen cutting
diagonally across the center of the drawing. In the upper center are docks
and the China Basin. At the lower right one can see Fort Funston and Lake Merced.

HILLS OF SAN FRANCISCO

Foreword by
HERB CAEN

Cover photograph: One of the most unusual city blocks in the world — Lombard street high on Russian Hill with its eight flower - bordered turns.

HILLS OF SAN FRANCISCO

This book was compiled from a series of articles which appeared in The San Francisco Chronicle.

Copyright, 1959, The Chronicle Publishing Company

Distributed by Nourse Publishing Company,
San Carlos, California

Hills of San Francisco

Foreword by HERB CAEN

"Take anything from us — our cable cars, our bridges, even our Bay — but leave us our hills."

This might well be the last rallying cry of the embattled San Franciscan, fighting to save his city — his unique, his beloved, his personal city — from the ever - increasing onslaughts of the manic-progressives, with their shopping centers, their housing projects, their freeways and their other plasticized examples of split-level thinking.

As the little boy said, holes are to dig — and, to the Grand Planner, hills are to be leveled. They are a luxury no right-minded mid-20th Century city can afford. They are difficult to build on. They are ruinous to traffic patterns. They are to be bored through, sliced off for whatever fill they afford, and finally eradicated as an affront to the orderly march of progress.(A hill is merely a thing of beauty — and mark my words well, Planner) a necessity to a San Franciscan.

For it is across its many mountains, crags and pinnacles that the city has lived the longest, sung the loudest and faced the winds of the future most courageously. From its hilltops, it has looked down on a burning city and vowed to rebuild even more magnificently. From the old castles on Nob Hill, it has shouted: "We are rich and strong, and there are no limits to what we can do." From the tiny wooden houses of Telegraph Hill, the many voices of the artist, the writer, the musician have carried to the ends of the earth. And from the windows of Twin Peaks and Potrero Hill it has gazed, with strange fondness, over the viewtiful city below and murmured "This is the only city, this is IT."

In San Francisco, the hills of home are — home.

"The citied hills," in Robert Louis Stevenson's well-turned phrase. As you prowl their various inclinations, you can feel the pulse of San Francisco and your own, both pounding with the beat of metropolis in action.

A tourist's goggled eyes as he inches up Powell Street on the cable, and the delighted shriek of a child on his first mad swoop down the Lombard Street curlycue — this is San Francisco. The old-timers walking backward up California Street (to conserve their breath while feasting on the vista of skyscrapers, Bay and bridge) and the trim secretaries pattering down Pine Street in sensible flat shoes (their spike heels are in their handbag, to be exchanged at the office door) — this, most emphatically, is San Francisco. Cabs scrambling like puppies up the Taylor Street precipice to the sharp edge of Nob Hill, kids whooping down the hushed side streets of Pacific Heights on home-made scooters (much more fun than Father's limousine), young lovers parked beneath Coit Tower and tearing their eyes away from each other to

watch a swollen moon rise unbelievably from behind the Bay Bridge — this, too, is San Francisco.

Of course, there are always the hard-bitten visitors who sneer, "I thought the hills would be steeper" (first cousin to the ones who look at the Pacific and shrug, "I thought it would be bigger"). These you deliver to the edge of the Filbert Street hill, with its 37.1 per cent grade, and, ignoring their yelps of "No! No!" drive down at full speed and to hell with the broken springs. If they faint dead away, so much the better, and when they recover, you can tell them about the more kindly tourist, who beamed: "I love this hilly city of yours. Whenever I get tired of walking around in it, I can lean against it!"

The hills — the tall and elegant, the fat and frowzy, the famous and infamous. Hills with wooden houses clinging desperately to their bony ridges, hills where blood has trickled down the bricks in scarlet rivulets, hills crowned with eucalyptus and alive with raccoons, hills where a poet named George Sterling exulted: "At the end of my streets are stars!"

Hills that are cleft in twain, hills that thrust rooftop saloons to uncharted alcoholic heights, hills transversed by tunnels. Hills that have disappeared — like Rincon, which lost its chic and then its head under the Bay Bridge approaches. Hills that are almost forgotten — like Sutro Heights, where a Mayor built his castle, strolled through a formal garden of European grandiloquence, and gazed at the ocean. Hills that are practically unknown — like Red Rock, where the young Saroyan sat, the wind ruffling his hair, and scribbled wild short stories in his notebook.

To some, there is only one hill—"The Hill" — Telegraph. To others, any hill is home, as long as it has a view. And to everybody in every section of the city, there is "Our hill," no matter how slight its eminence, no matter whether it has a name or not. In San Francisco, a hill need be no more than a state of mind, affording a slight rise to the spirits, a fresh outlook on the life that parades in the streets below.

According to the myth, San Francisco, like Rome, is built on seven hills — but which are the seven, and where? Barroom arguments have stormed far into the night over this issue, with never an answer; even the Public Library ducks the issue, and well it might.

For, as this book will disclose, San Francisco is built not on seven hills, or fourteen, or even twenty-one. The truth, as resolved by *The Chronicle's* intrepid crew of hill-climbers, is forty-two, each with its tradition, its history, its well-defined reason for being. And as you sit on your own particular hill — "THE hill," as far as you're concerned — I know you will be fascinated by stories of the other forty-one that rise all about you in the magnificent profusion of Baghdad-by-the-Bay.

Sutro Heights-An Ocean View

A WINDBLOWN GARDEN surrounded by strange battlements occupies Sutro Heights, one of the city's smallest, but best-known, hills.

From this vantage point, 200 feet above the Pacific, a visitor can view three miles of ocean beach to the south. He can look down on the Cliff House and across to Seal Rocks and north to Marin county. On a clear day, Mount Tamalpais is visible.

The garden, now a public park, has fallen into disrepair since the days when Adolph Sutro, German-born mining engineer and one-time (1895-97) Mayor of San Francisco, crated tons of fragile statuary around Cape Horn to the showplace he built after making a fortune in Nevada.

Many of the rather decayed statues remain, and the entrance, flanked by stone lions at Forty-eighth and Point Lobos avenues, is still

**Cross marks
Sutro Heights.**

The Cliff House has burned twice.

in use. So are the graveled central pathway and the other walks, and so are the ramparts from which visitors can watch ships steaming toward or from the Golden Gate.

The wild, wind-tortured cypress trees and the pines that attracted Sutro to buy the site are still thriving. Geraniums bloom most of the year, and old rose bushes are still nourished by the chill, damp ocean air.

But Sutro's home has disappeared. He built it in the 1880's, after he returned to San Francisco from the Nevada mines. The place was magnificent when he was alive, and his hospitality was renowned. The Heights, as it was known, was the scene of many fashionable parties and theatricals.

A corps of three gardeners and fifteen caretakers kept up the estate.

Sutro was so delighted with his place, in fact, that he invited the public to promenade in his garden. Picknickers and peanut munchers were barred — or at least they had to leave their baskets with a custodian — but all others were welcome from 9 a. m. to 5 p. m. daily.

In 1938, following the death of Sutro's daughter, Dr. Emma Sutro Merritt, the estate was turned over to the city. The following year, Sutro's once-magnificent home was razed.

A wispy fog lay over the Sunset District in this view of the Great Highway taken from Sutro Heights. In summer the beach is often jammed with swimmers braving the icy waters.

The city's unique skyline rises in this view from Rincon Hill, including the skyscrapers of

One of the Hills That Was

THIS IS A VIEW few San Franciscans, and certainly no tourists, ever see. It is a panorama of the city from Rincon Hill.

Rincon is one of the city's forty - two hills, and one with an old and distinguished history. The only trouble is, there's virtually nothing left of Rincon Hill. It has been cut and graded, lopped off and leveled; today its one - time summit is completely hidden beneath the spaghetti - like maze of concrete that marks the Bay Bridge approach and the northern tendrils of the downtown Freeway interchanges.

Rincon Hill covers the area roughly between Spear street and Second street, between Folsom and Brannan. It once was the most elegant neighborhood in town.

Crowded with magnificent mansions of residents who enjoyed virtually fog - free climate, it was far more substantial than the gaudier, *nouveau - riche* area of Nob Hill, across Happy Valley to the northwest.

On Rincon's southern slope was an equally fashionable block called South Park, built as an exact replica of London's Berkeley Square. It was staid and stuffy, the home of generals, bishops, and transplanted eastern capitalists.

Then came the grading projects. From 1866 on, one new street after another was cut into the hill. By the time of the fire, Rincon was a run - down region of boarding houses, seamen's hotels, bars and small factories.

Today, Rincon's gentle slopes house immense warehouses, the Key System tracks and a few reminders of seafaring days such as the Sailors' Union Building and the Apostleship of the Sea. The Union Oil Company tower dominates the skyline. South Park is still a small, genteel oval of greensward and trees, but the few residences around it are almost all slums, and most of the area is industrial.

The climate is still benign, however, and occasionally a stranger wanders into the old Rincon neighboorhood, to find a hint of the past in a decaying frame building, and a sense of the urgent present in a view of the city's skyline.

the business district, the Coit Tower on Telegraph Hill, and the Embarcadero freeway.

San Francisco --- Rincon

Cross locates
Rincon Hill.

This is Rincon Hill (in the foreground) as it looked before 1850, when only a few tents dotted its slopes. Across the center of town is Telegraph Hill.

Telegraph Hill
Goats to Glamor

THE VIEW through the eucalyptus trees is placid, but this word describes very little else about Telegraph Hill.

It has had an amazing variety of names — Loma Alta when the Spaniards first settled San Francisco, Windmill Hill in the 1840's after a mill was erected to grind coffee, and Signal Hill when a semaphore with big, black arms was built to announce the arrival of ships.

Then, in 1853, the lookouts atop the hill were replaced by watchers at Point Lobos who signaled word of arriving vessels to the hill's semaphore tower by Morse code. And thus the name, Telegraph Hill, was born.

It was a quiet, simple place, tenanted largely by goats and their keepers. Chileans lived at the base, and soon the Irish took over the summit. In the 1890's, Italians poured into San Francisco and won the hill.

Later came the artists, the poets, the writers and the people who wished they were writers. They now live chiefly on the less fashionable (and less expensive) landward slope of the hill in old, frame houses on obscure alleys. Some have been forced by rising rents to move to less romantic locations.

This colony, substantial at least in numbers, is considered by some to house the vanguard of a new literature in America.

And over the years have come the prosperous apartment dwellers who have built shiny new buildings, or remodeled old ones. They have brought plumbing and refrigerators and thick rugs to the hill.

Many consider this a recent movement, but a Chronicle article describing the hill in 1935 was headed, "Bohemians Edged Out." And ten years earlier, the last of the goats had been sent to even rockier pastures.

Most of the newcomers are eager to main-

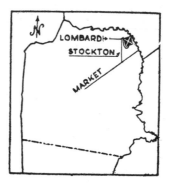

Cross marks Telegraph Hill.

tain the artistic tradition of the hill — as enjoyers, at least, if not participants. A great many are what Russell Lynes described some years ago as "Upper Bohemians" — people who make lots of money and live well, but who wear sports clothes to work and overalls for sport.

They, and the tourists who visit Coit Tower, share the finest of the hill's views. The right photo, snapped at the tower's base, shows the northern slope of Russian Hill, Golden Gate Bridge and the Marin cliffs at the outer Gate. Hidden behind a shrub to the left are the Church of SS. Peter and Paul, and North Beach. To the right are Fisherman's Wharf and Alcatraz.

Continuing around the hill to the right, the visitor can see Sausalito, Angel Island, the Campanile of the University of California at Berkeley, Treasure Island and the Bay Bridge. Closer at hand are the piers of San Francisco's harbor, the Embarcadero and the Ferry Building.

Next come the downtown office structures, starting with the square-topped Shell Building. Farther right is Union Square and the star-topped Sir Francis Drake Hotel. The eye takes in part of Nob Hill, including the Mark Hopkins and Fairmont hotels. And back again to Russian Hill and, perhaps, another stroll around the base of Coit Tower.

By now, the tower which rises 179 feet above the 284-foot hill, has become part of the city's scenery. But in the early thirties, there were desperate efforts to keep executors of the will of Mrs. Lillie Hitchcock Coit from erecting their fluted monument, completed in 1934.

The hill's newest monument, a 12-foot bronze statue of Christopher Columbus, was dedicated last year. Sculptor Vittorio de Colbertaldo came over from Italy to accept the city's congratulations and thanks for his work.

This tree-framed view of the Golden Gate was photographed from the base of Coit Tower on Telegraph Hill. At the foot of the hill is North Beach, Russian Hill rises at the left.

As this sketch shows, the old Telegraph Hill Observatory with its spectacular panorama, was a popular spot for carriage rides and promenades.

Lone Mountain
Island of Calm

LONE MOUNTAIN stands like an island of calm and serenity in the northwest section of the city.

Bypassed in the city's headlong rush across the barren sand dunes to the sea, it has never felt the hand of the subdivider or heard the call of the improvement association.

Its 448-foot height has been used almost exclusively for contemplation of one kind or another.

Today, its name is virtually synonymous with the single Catholic institution which commands its heights, the San Francisco College for Women.

Built in 1932 by the Society of the Sacred Heart, the graceful Spanish Gothic college now has more than 500 students, some 80 of whom are residents, and is still expanding.

The impression one gets of Lone Mountain, as he passes on a nearby street, is that of a place remote and apart from the city around it. On the north side, it simply looms up out of the bustle of outer Geary boulevard between Masonic and Parker streets.

Cross marks Lone Mountain.

On the other slopes, it presents beautifully lanscaped facades of green, broken only on the south by an elaborate stairway and entrance and exit gateways on Turk street.

How did it remain a place apart?

The city limits, as fixed by the Charter of 1851, ended at Larkin street, and everything beyond was known as "the outside land."

Land titles were much clouded in the Lone Mountain area, and, at that time, much of the sandy, windswept land was used only for cemetery purposes anyway.

When, in about 1860, the city attempted to straighten out this confusion, Bishop Joseph Sadoc Alemany, then Roman Catholic Archbishop, persuaded the city that full title should pass to the church for $8000.

In 1862, a huge cross was set up on the summit, a cross that could be seen by sailors at sea. It was succeeded by newer and larger crosses in 1875 and 1887, and the 1887 cross remained the only structure on the mountain until the building of the school.

At first, it was planned that the old cross would go atop the new buildings, but when it was dynamited out of the two tons of cement in which it was based, the cross proved too weathered and worm-eaten to go up again.

The college still hopes to make the loss good, however. In its plans for expansion is a splendid new chapel to rise on the very crest of the hill, and above the chapel a cross will rise to the old height which made it visible far out at sea.

For those who live, teach and study atop the mountain, one of the city's finest views is always available, a sweeping prospect from the Pacific to the Presidio and the towers of the Golden Gate Bridge, from the bridge to Sausalito across the bay and out across Pacific Heights to Alcatraz and beyond.

The camera looks past a teaching sister from the roof of San Francisco College for Women on Lone Mountain to Children's Hospital, Presidio Heights and the hills of Marin county.

This is the San Francisco College for Women, by itself atop Lone Mountain, and all but invisible from neighboring streets. The view from the top is one of the city's finest.

Corona Heights...
Hill With a Youthful View

ONE OF SAN FRANCISCO'S "youngest" hills in terms of recognition and distinction really belongs to the young.

For craggy, red-rocked Corona Heights looms so steeply above Sixteenth street and Roosevelt way — site of the city's junior museum — that only the young, the strong or the willing and able can climb its fenced, graveled walks to the top (official altitude — 510 feet).

But once there, the climber is rewarded with an unimpaired view to the east over the Bay, south over the Mission District, and northeast to downtown San Francisco.

Much of the hill's irregular contour can be attributed to a firm that operated a brick quarry and kiln on the southeastern slope of the hill for about 25 years, beginning at the turn of the century. The hill's red clay and rock furnished basic materials for "common brick."

The kilns collapsed into a molten mass during the 1906 earthquake. One pioneer contractor recalls using the melted kiln bricks for a colorful fireplace in his home.

"Rock Hill" was in sad shape after quarry and brick-making operations ceased.

But to Josephine D. Randall, San Francisco director of recreation, it was a potential site for a centrally located playground and nature museum for children.

Miss Randall, now a Palo Alto resident, surveyed dusty, dirty Corona Heights with James E. Phelan, recreation commission president, and other commissioners in 1928.

"We immediately became enthused about it," she recalled.

During the 1930's, WPA workers shored up the side of the hill to prevent landslides, and in 1936 San Francisco purchased a large portion of the 16-acre hillsite from the old Anglo National Bank affiliate, Consolidated Securities Company.

Four years later, the city had completed acquisition of the entire Corona Heights Playground site for $27,333.

In 1947, San Francisco voters passed a $12,000,000 bond issue for citywide recreational facilities.

But it took two more years to convince the Supervisors that the craggy, treeless hill was a better location for the nature museum than nearby Buena Vista Park.

Grading and construction began in late 1949, and the $345,000 Josephine D. Randall Junior Museum and Corona Heights Playground were formally dedicated by Mayor Elmer Robinson on September 23, 1951 — three months after Miss Randall had retired.

Grass and rock-covered Corona Heights looms high above Sixteenth street and Roosevelt way.

Corona Heights
location.

Quarrying and brick-making had cut severely
into the red-rocked slopes of Corona Heights
Hill as early as 1905,

It overlooks the Mission District (right) and
downtown San Francisco (left of center). The
road across its face leads to the right until it
reaches the Josephine Randall Jr. Museum.

View From Lincoln Heights

FAR ABOVE a rock-strewn shore, with wind-twisted cypresses bowing to leeward, Lincoln Heights rises 380 feet high between the outer Golden Gate and the more prosaic Outer Richmond.

Near the crest of the Heights, above Land's End, stands the Palace of the Legion of Honor, and on its inland slopes are the greens and fairways of Lincoln Park Municipal Golf Course.

Father Francisco Palou, founder and first celebrant of Mass at Mission Dolores, planted a cross on the highest point of the Heights in 1774.

Before the turn of this century, Father Palou's cross was gone, but around the site from 1867 to 1901 stretched acres and acres of cemetery land.

A potter's field, city burying ground for the homeless and unknown, stood in the sand heights, with poppies growing wild among the graves. There were other large plots for the many societies that grouped San Franciscans of diverse national origin — Italian, Greek, German, French, Scandinavian, Slovenian, Hebrew and Chinese.

A special tract of graves, looking out to sea, sheltered the remains of the early master mariners who had brought their schooners and clippers in through the Gate.

During this period, the local constabulary frequently had to patrol the Chinese area of the cemetery because of a unique custom that prevailed there. At Chinese funerals relatives of the departed left baked foods and other delicacies for the hungry spirits of the deceased, and when each funeral was over, the Skid Row denizens of the day would trek out through the sand dunes to feast on the sanctified offerings.

Now all that remains of the once-large burying ground on Lincoln Heights is a single crumbling relic of a Chinese temple. Its stylized gate, engraved with Chinese characters, rises above an empty, roofless crypt in a small clump of gnarled cypresses between the club-house and the first green of the golf course. The course itself was in development from 1903 to 1916.

The pride of Lincoln Heights, of course, is the Palace of the Legion of Honor, erected as a replica of its Paris counterpart by Alma de Bretteville Spreckels in 1924. The building honors California's dead of World War I, and is one of the Nation's leading art museums.

In front of the museum, little noticed by most visitors, stands a flagpole, the base of which bears an inscription denoting it as the western terminus of the great Lincoln Highway — the first Federal road from New York to California — which was conceived in 1912 when a transcontinental auto trip took up to forty days, and completed in 1930, when the same trip took four.

This is the Golden Gate, as seen from the Palace of the Legion of Honor, high atop Lincoln Heights. The road, El Camino Del Mar, skirts Lands End from Sea Cliff to Sutro Heights.

Site of Lincoln Heights.

Only this ruin of an old crypt remains from the once-crowded Lincoln Heights Chinese burial grounds. Now the 270 acres of Lincoln Park Golf Course cover the site, and the tree-shaded crypt is an odd trap for golfers.

Jail Gone, City College Took Hill

CITY COLLEGE HILL is an old landmark, but the name is new. For the college it was named after has been on its Balboa Park campus there for only seventeen years, and the institution has borne the title City College of San Francisco for just the last ten.

The school has replaced a disreputable old neighbor — the decrepit Ingleside Jail — in the southern part of the city. And the view that once was dimly visible through narrow, barred windows is now shared by more than 5000 students each day on the campus at Ocean and Phelan avenues.

The jail was a horrible place. In 1908, reformers protested that pairs of prisoners were forced to share cells 6 feet long, 4 feet 7 inches wide and 6 feet 6 inches high. The inmates included some distinguished former leaders of San Francisco, including Political Boss Abe Ruef and other turn - of - the - century figures.

The old wood and brick building near the hill's base was finally replaced in 1934, when the new San Francisco County Jail No. 2 was completed in the hills above San Bruno. Residents of the neighborhood celebrated the departure of the last prisoners by staging a program of music, sports and patriotic exercises.

Two years later, much of the park land was set aside for the new college, and in 1940 the campus was in operation.

The 350 - foot site, capped by the college's Science Building, offers a fine view. To the north there is Mount Davidson, topped by its great cross. The slopes of the hill below the cross are covered by the houses of the Sunnyside district and, farther to the left, Westwood, Westwood Highlands and Sherwood Forest.

The Pacific Ocean and, on very clear days, the Farallones, are visible to the west. Closer at hand, in much the same direction, are Riordan High School and the new Balboa Reservoir.

The view sweeps past Stonestown and Parkmerced southward to Westlake. And directly south lie the San Bruno Hills.

Immediately east of the campus, there is Balboa Park, with its tennis courts, baseball diamonds and clubhouse. Beyond the park, the view stretches toward the Cow Palace and Hunters Point.

**City College Hill
location.**

The front of City College's Science Building offers a peaceful view. To the north, rising above rows of residences, is Mount Davidson. To the west one can see Riordan High School.

The old Ingleside Jail was located for many years on the slope of what later became known as City College Hill. The aged relic was finally razed in 1934. This old sketch shows the jail and the buttressed wooden wall that surrounded it.

The view from Potrero Hill sweeps from Twin Peaks across Nob Hill with its apartment buildings and hotels, past downtown skyscrapers and the Civic Center to the Bay Bridge.

Potrero Hill: A Quiet Island in a Noisy Swirl of Traffic and Industry

POTRERO HILL was once a pasture for the cattle of nearby Mission Dolores. The name for both hill and district stems from just that — the Spanish word for stock grazing land.

Now the 300-foot-high hill, with its old houses and colorful Russian tradition, rises serene and detached above one of the busiest sections of the city.

Around its base swirl the freeway and the din and traffic of railroads, bridges, piers, warehouses and factories. But the sound of all this daily commerce diminishes as the steep streets rise, and vanishes on the peaceful crest.

The hill almost came by two different names. It was briefly called "Scotch Hill" because of Scottish boat builders and iron workers who came to live above the Union Iron Works when it was built in 1883.

Then, between 1904 and 1908, a group of Russian immigrants — fugitives from the Russo-Japanese War — settled there. But by that time, the city already had a Russian Hill.

The Russians are still deeply rooted in the hill and their heritage lends it a cosmopolitan and faintly exotic flavor. On a sunny afternoon one may see a group of old men sitting on kitchen chairs in a garage doorway — chewing over the day's events in their native language.

Or perhaps an elderly woman wearing boots, a shawl around her head, will cross the street on the way to her church, with its sign in Russian script.

The hill's population is varied, though, and includes many nationalities and races — most of them hard-working families in inexpensive homes.

There are some artists, too, and some refugees from Pacific Heights.

In fact, the hill is often described as being like the old Telegraph Hill — the way it was

**Cross marks
Potrero Hill.**

before its bohemian attraction drove out the goats and most of the painters.

On top of the hill, the houses are mostly old, frame ones, many with winding wooden front steps and a rakish Victorian charm. Some are ramshackle and dilapidated, showing the scars of weather and lack of care. But many others dazzle with their brightly painted doorways and multi-colored fences.

And aside from the view, which is most generous in its vista of bridges, hills and downtown buildings, residents are most proud of their weather, which they rank as best in the city.

For, situated as it is on the eastern flank of San Francisco, Potrero Hill often enjoys warm summer sun when the rest of the city is covered by fog.

The spirit of Old Russia still breathes on Potrero Hill. This old woman with her shawl, boots and cane was walking along Southern Heights when this photograph was taken.

Buena Vista's View Reaches Out

COVERED BY PINE, cypress and oak trees, Buena Vista Hill is said to be the site of San Francisco's "only natural park."

But its real distinction probably was recognized as early as the days of the Yerba Buena settlement. For *Buena Vista* means "good view" in Spanish.

The most dramatic sight from the hilltop is a relatively unimpaired view to the northwest — of the University of San Francisco, Lone Mountain, the top of Golden Gate Bridge. And beyond all these, the hills of southern Marin county.

To the south, hill climbers or motorists who drive to a comfortably large parking area atop Buena Vista can see nearby Corona Heights and sections of the Mission District.

But tree branches block the view of most of downtown San Francisco to the east and the Sunset District to the west. Some of the branches frame minute sections of these districts, but in these directions Buena Vista is more receptive to nature lovers than sightseers.

Credit for designating Buena Vista as a park dates to 1868, when San Francisco Surveyor Bill Humphreys laid it out as a park in a master plan for the expanding city.

The Committee on Outside Lands — arch opponent of numerous "squatters" of the day — placed Buena Vista's assessed valuation at $88,250, more than $2400 per acre.

And the Board of Supervisors formally designated the colorful, tree and bush-covered hill as a park on May 8, 1894.

Because of its steepness, height (569 feet above sea level), and foliage, Buena Vista permits no view of St. Joseph's Hospital and College of Nursing that are tucked on its eastern slope across Buena Vista drive.

And it's possible that scores of passengers who ride the N street car line have never stood on the hill they ride through for six minutes

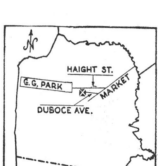

Cross marks Buena Vista.

daily (a three-minute trip each direction).

It was the Sunset (or Duboce) Tunnel that placed Buena Vista in the center of a bitter municipal controversy in the early 1920's.

Plans for the tunnel were promulgated in 1922, but many persons, particularly Mission District businessmen, came up with a proposal for an alternate route connecting downtown with the growing Sunset District. They advocated a tunnel through Mount Olympus.

This counter-proposal would have included facilities for auto and pedestrian traffic as well as street cars, but it died in 1924 when the affected property owners objected to tax assessments needed for its financing.

About that time, an organization known as the Sunset Transportation and Development Association revitalized the tunnel project through Buena Vista.

And the late Mayor James Rolph formally approved the $1,000,000 project on April 18, 1925.

After the city won several dramatic court battles, construction of the 4200-foot tunnel was started in June of 1926. It was finished in the month of October in 1928.

Today, visitors to Buena Vista are seldom aware that street cars are rumbling through the tunnel far below.

The winter of 1849.

The hills of southern Marin roll away beyond the trees of the Presidio. On the horizon, the slope of Angel Island blends into the tip of Marin county — Belvedere and Tiburon.

Thickly covered with trees, Buena Vista Hill stands as a gently curved mound of green against the horizon.

The View From Strawberry Hill

GOLDEN GATE PARK begins on the edge of the Pacific Ocean and rises steadily to a berry-shaped hill that commands it.

Strawberry Hill affords, for those who can and will climb by foot, a view that extends twenty-six miles out to the Farallone Islands on a clear day.

It commands the sweep across the blue path to the Golden Gate, the sea horizon from the Cliff House to the Zoo, and half a dozen interior views of the city's mosaic.

It commands surrounding Stow Lake and the dazzling horticultural history of the green park of which it is the center.

Those resolute ones who climb the spiraling path 412 feet to the summit scuffle their shoes on faded red bricks that bear the scars of the earthquake of 1906.

Until shaken to the ground by the quake, they helped support an elegant observatory which was a "Top o' the Mark" of the Nineties.

It was built by Thomas U. Sweeney, who landed here in 1852 with $15 in his pocket and squatted on some of the "Outside Lands"— 1013 acres of sand dunes, wild mustard fields and chaparral that later were sculptured into the park.

Sweeney profited nicely, and in 1890 gratefully donated funds for an observatory, which was constructed in the psuedo-classical fashion of the day.

The one-story edifice soon was overcrowded with picnicking, mustachioed men and their wives and children, and youths with bloomered girl friends.

Cross marks Strawberry Hill.

Sweeney handed the city more money. A second story, an outside balcony and a glass roof were appended and accepted with a fine oration by W. W. Stow, president of the Park Commission.

In the still-untamed park, the citizens left their dog carts, horse carts or bicycles by the lake side and mounted the hill in ever-increasing numbers.

First, they paused to admire Huntington Falls, which was given to the city by Collis P. Huntington, the railroad magnate. They admired, too, the black and white swans, geese, brant and wild duck of Stow Lake.

The surrounding park in those years rapidly was being changed into the genial jungle it is today, under the green thumb of a sandy-haired young Scot named John McLaren.

Artesian wells had been tapped and the water pumped to a reservoir on Strawberry Hill. The persistent Scot used the gravity power of the hill to irrigate *Ammophila Arenaria* (sand-loving sand grass), Australian tea trees and acacia, blue gum eucalyptus trees, manzanita, madrone and laurel, and a number of exotic grasses.

The wilderness was subdued.

Today "Sweeney's Panorama" invites Cub Scouts, the hardier students of the city, and couples in search of lofty solitude.

Below them, four million gallons of water daily keep the greenness; electric boats and aluminum canoes scud across the lake; and on the sea, ships approach the orange pillars of the Bridge.

Looking east over the tower of the de Young Museum, those who climb Strawberry Hill may see St. Ignatius Church and, just to the right, the outline of Mount Diablo.

Sweeney's Observatory was given to the city to show his appreciation for his rise from poor immigrant to prosperous citizen.

Hilltop of History...

MOST ANY VISITOR here will tell you that Lafayette Square is in Washington.

But San Franciscans who know their city will reply that Lafayette Square is ON Washington — and that it is at the crest of the hill that has been one of the city's big newsmakers.

News on the hill has been made by a famous squatter and working movie stars, members of the "old money" set and visiting Presidents who undoubtedly felt right at home living ON Washington and overlooking Lafayette Square.

News clippings on the hill go back to 1867, when the city acquired two crest blocks bounded by Laguna, Washington, Octavia and Sacramento streets, and designated them "Lafayette Square."

The same year, a former City Attorney, Samuel W. Holladay, claimed squatter's rights to another two square blocks at the hill's crest.

The city fought the claim in the courts, but Holladay, in 1870, built a white mansion, barn and windmill on the property. He lived there until 1915, when, at 91, his death occurred.

The legal battle for the land did not end until 1935, when the city finally purchased all but a small parcel of the Holladay property for $200,000. The sixty-year legal battle also gave Holladay immortality of a sort: The area around Lafayette Square has come to be called Holladay's Hill.

The Square, now bounded by Washington, Gough, Sacramento and Laguna streets, once was the site of the second astronomical observatory in California.

Cross marks the square.

Cresting Holladay's Hill is Lafayette Square, the expanse of lawns and trees at right. The Phelan and Spreckels mansions border the park. On the lower level at the left is the twin-turreted home of the California Historical Society.

Lafayette Square

It was erected at 378 feet above sea level in 1879 and was in use until 1907.

The building occupied by the California Historical Society at 2090 Jackson street was built in 1896 by the family of financier William Frank Whittier.

What about those movie stars?

They were among the hill's more recent news-makers. The palatial home of Mrs. Adolph R. Spreckels at 2080 Washington street was filmed in the movie "Pal Joey" as a night

In 1879 George Davidson built the second astronomical observatory in California atop the hill. The Davidson Observatory was in use at this site until 1907.

club frequented by Frank Sinatra, Rita Hayworth and Kim Novak.

The Square today is a grassy knoll where San Franciscans can gain luxurious views of the Marina and the Bay.

The mansions surrounding the Square are almost as luxurious as the view.

United States Senator, and former Mayor, James Duvall Phelan once lived in the mansion now occupied by Mrs. Felix S. McGinnis at 2150 Washington street. His guest book included such names as Paderewski, Tetrazinni, John McCormack and Theodore Roosevelt.

President and Mrs. William McKinley, in 1901, stayed for two weeks at the home of Henry T. Scott at 2129 Laguna street.

And it was in the same year that William C. Irwin, a Hawaiian sugar magnate, decided to build his mansion at 2180 Washington street. The $500,000 home housed the San Francisco Medical Society and the Irwin Memorial Blood Bank from 1926 to 1953. It was destroyed in 1956 by the sixty-foot flames of a three-alarm fire at dawn. Ruins were razed to make way for apartment houses.

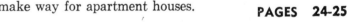

Medical Center on Parnassus

DOMINATING the skyline of Parnassus Heights are the clean, dramatic lines of the University of California's mammoth Medical Center.

The big buildings of the world - famous medical facility and the thousands of doctors, students, nurses, maintenance workers and patients that come to them also have a profound influence on life along the 400 - foot high ridge.

Many are the white jackets and starched aprons that can be seen each day in the bustle along Parnassus avenue.

And many are the residences in the area that let rooms to the hard - working students.

The white and gray concrete and steel medical buildings run along Parnassus Heights and are framed by the grays and greens of Sutro Forest's eucalyptus trees.

The forest and Mount Sutro tower behind the buildings. But north from Parnassus avenue, there is a handsome view that sweeps the Bay, Golden Gate Bridge, the Park, the Presidio, and looks almost directly down into Kezar Stadium .

To the east are quiet, residential streets that circle behind the medical center — Willard and Edgewood and Belmont avenues, rather like Berkeley.

Edgewood, a pretty lane lined with flowering Japanese plum trees, is one of the last brick - paved avenues in the city. Its houses back into the calm greenery of the forest.

Around to the north of Parnassus avenue plunges one of the two steepest streets open to traffic in San Francisco — Arguello boulevard between Carl street and Parnassus.

Present enrollment at the medical center totals 1290. Included in this figure are 245 medical students, 284 dental students, 135 student nurses and 266 pharmacy students.

Another 234 are physicians in internship and residency training.

During last year, there were 12,207 admissions to the Herbert C. Moffitt Hospital — not counting the 1543 babies born there.

The roots of the medical center go back to

1864, when Dr. Hugh H. Toland, a California pioneer, opened a small medical college in downtown San Francisco.

In 1873, Toland Medical College was deeded to the University as the first of the group of professional schools that comprise the San Francisco campus.

For those who look north from Parnassus Heights, there is a handsome view that sweeps out across the bay. And for those who look down, there is Golden Gate Park.

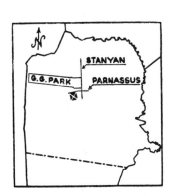

Cross designates Parnassus Heights.

The huge and sprawling buildings that comprise the University of California Medical Center dominate the 400-foot-high ridge of Parnassus Heights. Mount Sutro towers behind, framing the heights with the foliage of the eucalyptus trees of Sutro Forest.

Carved Crest at Candlestick Point

Just inland from Candlestick Point is the crest of Bay View Heights. Atop the hill is the **KYA transmitter. This picture was taken from Ward and Goettingen streets to the west.**

INITIALLY SOUGHT as a pest house site, transformed into a city park and now heading into an uncertain future is one of the most impressive hilltops in old San Francisco — Bay View Heights.

The crest, inland from Candlestick Point, remains 500 feet above the bay, but there is a possibility that in the near future it may be cut down to less than half that height.

Nearly a century ago part of the hill and much land to the north were owned by the Bay View Land Company, formed by George Hearst, father of the late William Randolph Hearst, to develop what was expected to become a very exclusive district.

"They had a horse car operating out there in 1864," said Lou Jolly, early resident, historian and improvement club representative of southeastern San Francisco. "But nothing much ever came of the development. It was too far out, and Butchertown started moving in, about 1869 or 1870 . . ."

There also was a very fine small boat harbor just north of Bay View Heights, Jolly recalled, and by the 1880's several pioneer families were grazing cattle around the slopes of the hill. One of the better known: Jacques Sarthou, "who started bringing in cattle around 1860, I think."

Part of the crest, which now is municipally

Architect's scale model for the new baseball stadium on Bay View Heights.

owned, was purchased by the city from the Bay View Land Company in December, 1902, Recreation and Park Department records show. And a dozen years later the abortive pest house project there resulted in city acquisition of the remainder of the land now forming Bay View Park.

The estate of Charles Crocker — which still owns approximately 3700 acres of land in the area — gave its ridge acreage to the city on condition that the proposed "pest house site" be made into a park instead.

"The estate didn't want any pest house (isolation hospital) that close to its other lands," one city official explained.

As a result, the hilltop was finally dedicated for park purposes on December 8, 1915.

In addition to the park, the hill also is adorned by KYA's radio transmitter tower and, during election years, usually bears the name of a candidate in huge white letters. The south slope is not city owned; it belongs to the scavenger company which is taking part of the earth for garbage covering operations.

North and east slopes also are being carved away by their

Cross marks Hill.

owner, Contractor Charles L. Harney, to develop San Francisco's major league baseball stadium.

"The park is going to be a pretty steep-sided island, and the problem now is whether to keep the park up there or grade the whole hilltop down to a lower level," a member of the City Planning Commission staff explained.

The Hunters Point Reclamation District reported last year that if the 500-foot-high park were cut down to 190 feet, enough economical fill would be produced to reclaim 250 acres of tidelands.

A spokesman for the San Francisco Recreation and Park Department, however, said: "There will still be an easy access road to the hilltop from the west — Harney is required to leave that — so we don't see any necessity for cutting down the hilltop . . ."

Steep-sided or not, he said, the park as it stands contains some attractive trees and some interesting rock formations.

Already long gone, of course, is the original candelabra-shaped rock formation down on the point which gave Candlestick Point its name.

Hill With History...and a Future

A hiker proceeding almost due north from the Cow Palace will encounter the wild, 515-foot-high McLaren Ridge and its pristine heights, reminiscent of Alpine meadows. When the park

ALL OF THE CITY'S HILLS throw their shadows on areas of remarkable history. McLaren Ridge, too, is ringed with history.

But, more than all the hills, it dwells in the future.

Soon its two rugged green humps will crest the second largest park in San Francisco, which was a dream of John McLaren during the years in which he turned gusty dunelands into Golden Gate Park.

These 326 acres at the southeastern gates to the city already are named for the late Scottish horticultural architect. But their wild heights — they rise to 515 feet — will be left somewhat untamed; McLaren wanted the people to have unspoiled Alpine joy even within the city.

The dream of John McLaren has almost hardened into reality — but only after more than three decades of frustration. Despite opposition, the city has kept buying land parcels and now is building a $409,000 swimming pool. Construction of a nine-hole golf course will begin this summer.

Northwest of the park, in the Bayview District, lies another great piece of the future; the site of a $15,000,000 stadium for the San Francisco Giants. Perhaps one day the cheering at a World Series will ring across the ridge.

If you look due east, you see the mighty cranes of Hunters Point Naval Shipyard. Here, a century ago, pioneer settlers held clambakes on the picnic grounds of John and Jacob Hunter.

Just to the south is the region once known as La Visitacion. Herds from Mission Dolores were kept here.

If you hike down the steep slope to Sunnydale avenue and walk toward the San Mateo county line, you will see, near Bayshore boulevard, the home built by Peter Burnett, first American Governor of California, when he moved here from San Jose.

Nearby lives Charles A. Louis, 84, who opened the Reis Tract in 1904 and sold lots at $125 each, $1 down and $1 a week.

During the earthquake and fire of 1906, he says, hundreds of families fled into the unshaken valley and lived in tents.

is completed, the ridge will remain untamed.
At right, a water tower beside a reservoir.

X shows McLaren Ridge

Below the ridge nestles Visitacion Valley, sheltered also by
the hills of Bayview Park. Beyond is Candlestick Point.

Quiet Park Has Violent History

ALAMO HILL was just another rocky summit along the winding trail from Mission Dolores to the Presidio in San Francisco's earliest days.

But the city grew around it, squatters pitched tents and built hovels on its slopes, and just a century ago the 225-foot hill was officially declared a public park by the State Legislature. Its name became Alamo Square.

Today it is a pleasant slope with widespread lawns, tennis courts and clusters of evergreens, palms and eucalyptus. Oldsters play chess in hedge-sheltered nooks and sunbathers relax there on fair days.

Nothing in Alamo's quiet mien these days betrays its raucous, violent history, when squatters battled for its land and legal wrangles implicated platoons of city officials in charges of corruption.

Alamo Square is bounded by Fulton, Scott, Steiner and Hayes streets. From its steeply sloping summit there is hardly a trace of marine view in any direction, for the square is surrounded by other hills — Pacific Heights to the north; Buena Vista Park and Parnassus Heights to the south and southwest; Lone Mountain to the northwest. Eastward, where the distant view once encompassed the entire bay, the sight of water is walled off by the tall buildings of the downtown business district.

Old Alamo Hill's most famous — and disreputable — citizen was Charles P. Duane, a Tipperary bucko who wenched and fought and politicked around the city in the middle 1850's.

He was convicted of assault in 1851, fi-

Cross marks Alamo Square.

nagled himself a pardon, and won election as chief engineer of the city's volunteer fire department in 1852.

Four years later he was caught stuffing a ballot box and was exiled from San Francisco under pain of death by the Vigilance Committee.

From 1854 on, Dutch Charley Duane, a powerful member of the City Hall Muggins Club, had claimed squatter's rights to all of Alamo Hill. He fought bare-fisted against other squatters, and when he returned from exile in 1860 he took his claim for the valuable land to court.

The land had become a public park in 1858, but Charley persuaded the Board of Supervisors to refrain from rejecting his claim. There were hassels and outcries; there was a gunfight at City Hall in which Duane slew Colonel William G. Ross — and later won a dubious acquittal. Finally in 1877 Charley lost his squatter's case in the courts. Ten years later he was dead.

Alamo Square itself, during all this time, was a rocky wasteland frequented by the bonfire-building, pigeon-potting youths of Hayes Valley. Jim Corbett, climbing up the hill from his father's livery stable, was the acknowledged king of the mountain long before he became Gentleman Jim, king of the boxing ring.

But in 1892 civilization came to Alamo Hill. The city spent $25,000 grading and landscaping it. The kids and squatters left, and except for a few hectic weeks in 1906, when 1000 refugees from the fire tented on its ground, the square has been a sedate park ever since.

The pleasant slopes of Alamo Square, rising from Hayes Valley, command an urban view.

Tall buildings from Pacific Heights to Market street block off almost all view of the bay.

Refugees from the 1906 fire found safety and temporary homes on the summit of Alamo Hill.

CHARLEY DUANE
Squatter's rights.

Private Lives on Forest Hill

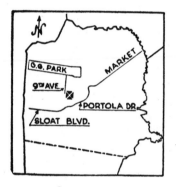

FOREST HILL rises to the west of Sutro Forest and Twin Peaks. It is a gentle slope with grassy, tree-lined walkways, spacious homes and a quiet, self-contained air of solid, prospering family life.

Like St. Francis Wood, it was one of the first tracts developed in the western part of the city with the completion of the Twin Peaks tunnel. And in 1912, the tract promoter described Forest Hill in the following fine prose:

"It is a place of real homes, individual of location and taste, so set and sheltered that one man's garden is not his neighbor's observatory . . .

"A place of woodland aisles and woodland quiet, serene in the very heart of the metropolis."

One early resident of the area recalls seeing rabbits and quail scurrying through wild lupine on the hillside when he first moved in. The animals, of course, departed as soon as San Francisco began growing up around the area, but much of the verdant beauty remained. There are Irish elms, hawthorn, pines, eucalyptus and acacia along the streets.

Forest Hill's streets, however, have never been accepted by the city, and, as a result, the Forest Hill Association, formed in 1917, keeps them up, sweeps them and waters the parking strips.

The association also has its own clubhouse and rents the premises for weddings, community dances, Girl Scout and garden club meetings.

Each resident of the hills pays a small fee for the upkeep services provided by the association.

Architecture on the hill is varied, to say the least, running a wide range from heavy Tudor through early American colonial to modern functionalism with its spartan angles and cubes.

The top of the hill is about 700 feet, cresting somewhat above the intersections of Ninth and Mesa avenues.

On the summit is a water tank, and from this point there is a sweeping view of the Sunset District, Ocean Beach and the Pacific Ocean to the west.

Most of the residents look out from the east side of the hill to the hills and ridges at the city's center.

Forest Hill is bounded by Laguna Honda and Dewey boulevards, and directly before it sprawls the complex that is the Laguna Honda Home for the aged.

Cross marks Forest Hill.

Laguna Honda Home for the Aged.

Looking north from Forest Hill, the sweeping view takes in Sutro Heights (right) and Golden Gate Heights (center). In the distance are the park, bay, Angel Island and Marin county.

San Marcos avenue on Forest Hill illustrates the sylvan atmosphere and variegated architecture that so mark the area.

Laurel: a Hill for the Living

MORE THAN 100 years ago, San Francisco's "Gold Rush" pioneers laid out their cemetery plots on the gentle slopes of Laurel Hill.

Beneath its pines and oaks and willows were the graves of such notables as Andrew Smith Hollidie, inventor of the cable car; Dave Scannell, first Sheriff of San Francisco; a son of Napoleon Bonaparte, and countless other early settlers on the bay.

Today, Laurel Hill's 54 acres ring with the laughter of children and the cacophony of auto horns, door slams, barking dogs.

Attractive stucco and frame homes appear in tightly knitted bunches along winding streets that once were peaceful burial grounds.

It took more than 40 years of sporadic legal battles to overcome opposition to the removal of the dead and bring on the bulldozers that were to clear the hill for the living.

Bounded on the north by California, the south by Geary, the west by Parker and the east by Presidio, Laurel Hill is in the very heart of residential San Francisco.

Napoleon Bonaparte's son was buried here.

Development of the site into a multi-million-dollar residential subdivision didn't get under way until after World War II.

The city purchased a huge section overlooking Masonic with the idea of building a high school. Later, another location was decided upon and the city sold the land to the Fireman's Fund Insurance Co.

Fireman's did the tract proud, erecting a superb, sprawling building of modernistic design that rules the hill's easternmost portion.

On the west side of the hill are the homes and apartments, with carefully manicured lawns ending in steep, short banks.

The area, zoned for second residential, has a comfortable, though bustling, atmosphere today that gives not the slightest hint of its historic beginning.

Cross marks Laurel Hill.

Looking toward the north across the intersection of Masonic and Euclid avenues on 54-acre Laurel Hill, now one of the city's newest and most bustling residential areas.

More than 100 years ago, Laurel Hill's gentle slopes served as a cemetery for San Francisco's "Gold Rush" pioneers.

Russian Hill: Steep, Green Home Place

HIGH IN the northeastern corner of San Francisco between North Beach and Pacific Heights rises Russian Hill. It is a hill of shaft-like apartment buildings, fine homes, splendid views, hidden cottages, frame flats and verdant gardens. It is the hill of the board chairman and of the stenographer. It is the home white-collar workers go to when the downtown offices close.

No one knows for sure how Russian Hill got its name. The Spaniards ignored the hill because of its inaccessibility. So did the first Yankee settlers. Then came the Russian seal hunters, led by the romantic Count Rezanov.

The Russian sailors buried their dead at the crest of Vallejo street because the hard clay remained firm, unlike the sand on the summits of other hills. Later, so the most likely story goes, American children, playing among the graves, began to use the name Russian Hill.

For many years, the hill remained a goat pasture, covered with wild mustard — a yellow blanket, three feet thick. In 1852 it was officially recognized by the name Russian Hill when thousands turned out to witness the city's first legal execution — the hanging of Jose Forni for murder.

William Penn Humphries, an old Indian fighter, built the first house on the hill in 1852 on the northeast corner of Chestnut and Hyde streets. Captain David Dobson erected an observatory tower nearby and charged 25 cents for a view that could be had for free. The city's first octagonal house still stands at 1067 Green street.

The hill today remains a place apart, of quiet charm, where steps climb crazily through greenery and brick-flagged lanes wind up sheer heights. The height is capped with eucalyptus trees, iron oak and pine.

The hill, bounded roughly by Bay, Columbus, Powell, Pacific and Polk streets, crests in a dogleg running from north to east. The hill contains two tiny gems of parks — Coolbrith at Vallejo and Taylor streets, and an unnamed plot at Lombard and Larkin streets.

On a tile bench in the latter park there is a plaque dedicated to the late George Sterling, poet and leader of Bohemia.

There, among the sycamores and cypress, Russian Hill mothers take their babies to sit in the sun. They listen to the rush of the leaves and the rattle of the Hyde street cable and look out over the Marina to the Golden Gate and the sea beyond.

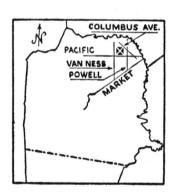

Cross marks Russian Hill.

This photograph taken in 1870 shows the city's first octagonal house, which still stands on Green street. From the cupola there was a direct view of the Bay and East Bay hills.

This is the bottom of one of the windingest city streets in the world — Lombard street between Hyde and Leavenworth, with eight flower-lined turns in the one block.

The view from the park high on Russian Hill includes a characteristic old house, the Bay and the Golden Gate Bridge with the hills of Marin.

The Good-Natured Gardeners of Anza Vista

MIDDLE - AGED COUPLES, most of whom have raised families and now relax evenings tending their gardens or manicuring picture - book lawns, predominate on Anza Vista Hill.

This is a comfortable, civic - minded neighborhood ready to speak its mind on public issues (it has, on notable occasions), or boast good - naturedly of its beautiful gardens and homes.

One of its streets — Anza Vista avenue — is one of the most peculiar in San Francisco. It forms a triangle, adding a novel touch that residents over the years have learned to appreciate and wouldn't have any other way.

Anza Vista School, pastel - green and sprawling, was built on the western slope of the hill eight years ago, although residents argued with the school board at the time that this wasn't the place for it. With few young couples around, there aren't many school - age children in the neighborhood.

Amateur horticulturists, who will try just about anything once, abound on Anza Vista. Some have even changed the complexion of the landscape with their experimental green - thumbing, persuading bunches of Kentucky bluegrass to thrive.

Zoning is mixed, with first and second, single and multiple dwellings.

This tract was developed eleven years ago from the old Calvary Cemetery. Located on the northernmost boundary of Geary street is a modern Sears store of three levels, and adjacent to it, handsome Kaiser Foundation Hospital.

Turk street to the south, Masonic to the west and St. Joseph to the east enclose the subdivision.

The hill, on a clear day, affords its western residents a view of the Golden Gate Bridge and parts of Marin county; from the east can be seen the University of California and the Berkeley hills; from the southerly end of the tract there is a peek far down toward San Mateo county.

The hill and its triangle - shaped central street trace their name to the intrepid Spanish soldier, Juan Bautista de Anza. He led the first immigrants from Mexico into San Francisco in 1775.

**X marks
Anza Vista Hill.**

Architect's drawing for the Anza Vista Elementary School which was built in 1950.

This view of Anza Vista Hill, looking west on O'Farrell from Broderick, shows the modern

Kaiser Foundation Hospital, overlooking Geary street. Behind it: a big Sears, Roebuck store.

Juan Bautista de Anza.

Back in the Thirties, when Anza Vista Hill was still Calvary Cemetery, an old woman — she always refused to identify herself — spent hours walking among the graves or resting on the steps of the monuments. She said she wanted to be with her "old friends."

Dolores Heights' Own Spectacular

Back IN 1776, when the Franciscan Fathers were picking a site for the Mission of St. Francis, the Indians told them the best climate and purest water were to be found at a hill about three miles inland.

The fathers recognized a choice spot when they saw it, and founded their new mission next to a small lake fed by the streams from the hill, with plenty of good pasture land for their cattle on the grassy slopes.

Today, the lake is gone — replaced by Mission High School. And the hillside pasture land was long ago covered by houses, their foundations chipped into the solid red rock underneath.

But, as any resident of Dolores Heights (or Noe Hill) will proudly tell you, the balmy, fog-free climate is still there.

The Mission still sits at the foot of the hill.

And the spring water is still there, too, trickling down the rocky cuts above Sanchez and Liberty streets and the other goat paths that were blasted into roads over the hill.

Added to the superb climate is one of the most spectacular views of the city to be found anywhere.

For years the hill was used as grazing land, part of the rancho of Don Jose de Jesus Noe, last Mexican *alcalde* of Yerba Buena.

One of the first homes on the heights was the stately mansion of Adolf Scheerer, a contractor from Germany, who moved to the hill in the 1880's from a house at Post and Taylor streets, on the site of the Bohemian Club.

The materials for Scheerer's mansion — which is still standing at 450 Liberty street — had come 'round the Horn, but hauling them up the steep face of Dolores Heights, by chains and mules, was almost as big a task as the trip from the East.

Scheerer furnished the grounds of his new home with statuary from Woodward's Gardens, a famous resort and museum at Thirteenth and Mission streets.

Sheep and goats still grazed on the slopes around the big house and down among the gravestones of the Jewish cemetery (where Mission Park now is).

In the Nineties, the hill attained a certain popularity as a spa, with the discovery of a well with supposedly beneficial waters in the back yard of a house at the very top of the hill (at the southwest corner of Twenty-first and Sanchez streets; altitude 360 feet).

The curative powers of the well water were doubted by many, but even today the story is told that gold was found in the craws of ducks that drank the water.

The well eventually was filled in — after the lady of the house fell in and was drowned.

In 1906 the springs of Dolores Heights provided much of the fresh water for the earthquake-devastated city. The Army set up tents in Mission Park (the cemetery having been moved some years earlier) and hundreds of refugees camped there.

In the early years of this century, Dolores Heights was known throughout San Francisco as "Battle Mountain."

Residents of the hill fought bitterly over location of the streets the city was preparing to cut into the sides of the hill. Everyone wanted the paved street to be at the level of his house — not that of the house across the way, which might be twenty or thirty feet higher or lower.

The scars of the battle still are visible in the high retaining walls and steps outside some homes — and the compromise that left parts of Sanchez and Liberty streets on two different levels.

Perhaps the fanciest of houses and cottages stuck to the side of the hill is the one built in 1930 by Sunny Jim Rolph, long-time Mayor of the city.

Set up as an entertainment hideout by the gregarious Rolph the house is on

Cross marks the hill.

San Francisco sparkles in spectacular fashion in this night photograph taken from the Joseph

Salomon home, built by the late Sunny Jim Rolph, atop the hill. (Ex.: 3 minutes, f.11.)

the northeast corner of Sanchez and Twenty-first streets, almost hidden among dozens of trees of every description.

The trees were saplings from Golden Gate Park, planted under the supervision of the park's superintendent, John McLaren. Holes four feet across and sixteen feet deep were gouged out of the red rock for each tree.

When Rolph went to Sacramento as Governor, he gave the house to his son, James Rolph III, who lived in it for a short time. It now belongs to Joseph Salomon, president of a local tanning firm.

The Adolf Scheerer home, built of materials brought around the Horn in the Eighties, was one of the first houses built on the heights.

S.F.'s Traditional Socialite Ridge

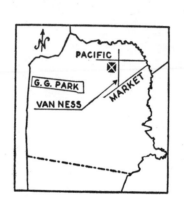

PACIFIC HEIGHTS IS, topographically speaking, not a hill, but a ridge, with all the peaks and valleys that were distinctive features of the area in the sand-dune days of a century ago, now lost for the most part to the bulldozers of progress.

Its boundary, according to the California Historical Society's librarian, James Abajian, who found it spelled out in the 1893 city directory, is California street to Broadway, between Van Ness and Fillmore.

From an upper floor view window of an apartment house, the Marina looks far below, but Pacific Heights at its loftiest, Lafayette Square, is only about 385 feet above sea level.

Various periods in the city's history have seen the so-called "most fashionable district" change from eminence to eminence (Rincon to Nob, for instance). Today, and for many decades, Pacific Heights has held that distinction; there probably are more socialites per square block here than in any of the other districts of San Francisco.

From the summit of the ridge, which runs between Pacific avenue and Broadway, Pacific Height slopes gently southward, but falls away sharply to the Marina on the north. And from the drawing rooms of the mansions you get a sweeping view of the bay, the Golden Gate and the Marin hills.

Not until the first cable car went over Nob Hill and on outward in 1878 did builders see any possibilities in this district.

Before then it was a pretty wild area, where were located a few lonely duck ranches and dairy farms. It was a favorite spot for hunters, hikers and nature lovers. Hikers particularly liked to climb around a huge outcropping called

**Pacific Heights
location.**

Black Rock, near what is now Pacific and Broderick.

In the early days, a steam train rolled down Baker street and past a marshland (now the Marina) to Harbor View (now Yacht Harbor), scene of salt water baths, clambakes, steam beer parties and picnics.

One of the hills of those days, no longer on any map of San Francisco, was Gulliver's Hill, described by one historian of the time, as situated "a good ways out on the Presidio road." The Presidio road itself was a winding affair, a planked toll road.

Gulliver's Hill, in the neighborhood of present Green and Webster streets, was named after Captain Charles Gulliver, a "milk rancher and good hunter who had the finest quail, duck and rabbit shooting in San Francisco."

One of the valleys was Cow Hollow. This is popularly thought to be the Marina, but old records indicate it lay north of Vallejo street and west of Van Ness.

Great mansions rose on the heights. Tall apartment houses have in recent years made inroads into this fashionable district, but many of the showplaces still stand — among them Alma de Bretteville Spreckels' place on Washington street, and in the next block the huge place built by Senator James D. Phelan, and the Flood home on Broadway that is now the Sacred Heart School for Girls.

The California Historical Society itself is now housed in one of those mansions, the Whittier place, an elegant Victorian red sandstone residence at 2090 Jackson street, built in 1894-96. It boasted an innovation of the day — closet lights that turned on when you opened the doors.

This is the imposing Spreckels mansion on Washington street. Apartments in the area boast rosters of residents that read like a San Francisco edition of the Social Register.

Pacific Heights, as it looked in 1857, with Cow Hollow (left) and the old Presidio road.

In 1864 steam trains rolled down Baker street through the swamps to what is now the Marina.

A Hill That Couldn't Live Up to It's Name

ONE OF THE LEAST known of San Francisco's hills is University Mound — but it might have been one of the best known.

The area, north of what is now McLaren Park and ten blocks west of the Bayshore Freeway, was obtained by the city in the last century as the proposed site for a city college.

In anticipation, the nearby streets were named after Oxford, Cambridge, Goettingen, Harvard, Yale, Princeton and other schools thought to be worth emulating.

But the city failed to follow through and no walls meant for ivy rose on the site until 1863, when the Presbyterians established the University Mound College there.

This was a boarding school branch of the church's downtown City College. Total enrollment for the first year of the branch: four students.

The site, with the gentle, symmetrical slope of an Indian burial mound, made an ideal campus, but the college failed to prosper. University Mound rises to a height of 265 feet at Cambridge and Burrows streets.

Before the school's doors were entirely closed to education, however, it had a brief but noisy career as the University Mound Institute and Boarding School for Boys. This lasted from 1869 to 1871.

James Lick, San Francisco multimillion-

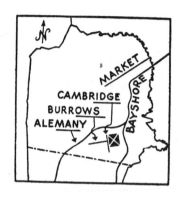

Cross marks University Mound.

aire, bought the twenty-five acre property in 1871, just five years before he died, and left a $3,000,-000 bequest to the city.

The three-story frame school building was transformed into the James Lick Old Ladies Home, since renamed the University Mound Old Ladies Home.

The home, a nonprofit, nonsectarian institution, now houses sixty-eight elderly women. They live in an attractive Georgian brick structure built in 1932 after the old building was torn down.

The home fronts on a city reservoir. On the heights above it is the University Mound Training School for Girls, operated by the Sisters of the Good Shepherd.

The training school for delinquent girls was constructed in 1932 on the upper half of the James Lick property. Now one hundred and thirty-five girls reside in six Spanish-style residences surrounding the classroom building and convent.

In addition to the training school and old ladies home, University Mound is noted for the hothouses and nursery gardens on its slopes. The district specializes in the cultivation of orchids, carnations and roses.

So, with the blue water of its reservoir, its gardens and its stately brick buildings, University Mound could be mistaken for the major college campus it failed to become.

The gentle slope of University Mound often goes unnoticed among the city's more spectacular hills. The big building just behind covered reservoir is University Mound Old Ladies' Home.

This is how the old University Mound College looked before it was demolished.

Sunset Panorama From Larsen's Peak

CARL G. LARSEN had a fey feeling for sand dunes. He made very good ham and eggs. These facts have a great deal to do with the birth and growth of a pleasant residential area in the Sunset District called Golden Gate Heights.

Golden Gate Heights has one of the finest views to be seen in a city of fine views.

Larsen made a packet in the days before this century turned by selling ham and eggs at his Tivoli Cafe near the old Tivoli Opera House on Eddy street. His guests included the elect of the American theater — Forrest, Augustin Daly, William Gillette, Tyrone Power the elder, and young Jack Barrymore.

The canny Dane, who came here from the old country in 1869, used to top his menu with the legend: "Fresh eggs from Tivoli

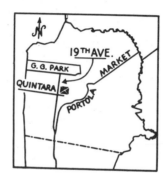

Cross marks Golden Gate Heights.

Cafe Ranch every day." That ranch is known today as Sunset Heights Park. Or, sometimes, Larsen's Peak, elevation 725 feet.

With the money he made from breakfasts he bought up big gobs of what one of his contemporaries called "that great stretch of shifting sands and sagebrush south of the park." His dream was to convert his four square miles of dune hills into "the tropics of the San Francisco hills."

He very nearly did it. Single-handed he created the residential area known as Golden Gate Heights, a proud little hilltop community splashed with lilacs and begonias and even a vagrant palm or two.

Several years before his death in 1928, at the age of 84, Larsen deeded to the city 250,000 square feet, or six acres, of property sit-

The sweeping beauty of the view from Golden Gate Heights is seen in this picture from Larsen's Peak. Larsen deeded the land to the city for use as a park during the Twenties.

uated between Twelfth and Fourteenth avenues and Quintara and Pacheco streets.

It was from this eminence that the pictures above were taken.

Larsen started buying Sunset District dunes in 1888. His friends thought him a bit mad. But he died packed with pelf, and not all of it from eggs.

Two years after he bequeathed the area now known as Sunset Heights Park to the city, he gave another two city blocks for a park and children's playground.

The tract, on Nineteenth avenue between Ulloa and Wawona streets, was named Carl G. Larsen Park in his honor. Larsen never married. He gave the park as a legacy to the children of San Francisco. It is remembered and used as such.

Ironically, his first gift, in its beautiful situation overlooking the city, is neglected, overgrown and squalid with weeds. A tennis court is almost never used. The children Larsen thought so much of have other things to do.

Larsen's Park, given to the city for children, is now largely unused and weed-covered.

The Modest Summit Most People Overlook

CASTRO HILL probably is the most overlooked hill in the city.

Every year thousands of sightseers look right over it to downtown San Francisco and the Bay from the lookout points on Portola drive and Twin Peaks. Castro Hill, 500 feet below the peaks, fades into an insignificant part of the foreground.

In the other sense of the word, Castro Hill was for years overlooked as a place to live. As late as 1901, pictures show that few people had figured out a compelling reason for building homes on the steep, barren hilltop just east of Twin Peaks on Twenty-second street.

It was hardly more developed than in the 1850's, when it was part of the ranch of Don Jose de Jesus Noe. (The big ranch house was down in the sheltered valley at the western base of the hill, about where Alvarado Elementary School now stands at Douglass and Alvarado streets.)

Yet once people did build homes on Castro Hill, they found it well worthwhile.

Consider the view from the 407-foot summit (at the end of Collingwood street, just north of a hairpin turn on Twenty-second street):

To the north, Buena Vista Heights and the hills of Marin county; to the northeast, the breathtaking skyline of downtown San Francisco and the Bay Bridge; to the east, Potrero Hill, the Bay and Mt. Diablo; to the south, Diamond Heights and the San Bruno Mountains, and, every evening, sunset behind Twin Peaks.

Castro Hill rears right up between two of the city's finest sun traps — Noe Valley to the south and Eureka Valley to the north. As such it shares in the "warm belt" climate.

The fog that moves in on the Sunset District all summer and spills over Twin Peaks seldom reaches as far as Castro Hill.

The only climatic drawback, in fact, is the brisk, prevailing west wind that hits the exposed hilltop, necessitating fences or other windbreaks along the western property lines. (Castro Hill itself is a natural windbreak for the residents of Dolores Heights, three blocks east and forty-seven feet lower.)

The hill was developed too recently to boast any famous landmarks, and its inhabitants have behaved themselves well enough to avoid the kind of newspaper stories that nurture legends.

The only historic-appearing building on Castro Hill turns out to be a practical joke. Perched right on top of the peak is a fortress-like stone building with a high stone wall complete with peepholes. It looks at first glance like an old mission, well fortified against attack.

But it is only a homemade house, built about twenty years ago by someone with unlimited access to the paving stones that were being replaced by asphalt and concrete on the city's streets. The forbidding wall is nothing more than a defense against the west wind. (The peepholes were an unexplained whim of the builder.)

Cross marks Castro Hill.

The hill's one claim to historical fame is that it was the location of the only cable car line south of Market street. The ivory white cars used to rumble all the way out from the Ferry Building to Castro and Seventeenth streets (the end of Market street). Then they would turn south onto Castro street and run out as far as Twenty-sixth.

After the earthquake, the cables were removed from Market street, and the Castro cable line started at Eighteenth street. Having no tourist trade at all to justify its retention, the line passed quietly into oblivion during World War II. The lack of historic past doesn't bother the people who live on Castro Hill, though. They are content with their view, their gardens and their sunshine. Most of them don't even know their hill has a name (conferred on it by the Planning Commission in 1939). They refer to it simply as "the hill," or, if pressed for something more specific, "the hill I live on." It's as good a name as any.

1958—Looking down Twentieth street toward Castro Hill, you see a mixture of the old and the new. New neighbors have joined old houses and the street is now paved.

1901—Some thirty-eight years after this photograph was taken, the ridge in the left middle distance was officially named Castro Hill by Planning Commission.

Mt. Sutro---Nature Was Revamped to Save San Francisco

THE CITY'S THIRD - HIGHEST HILL has saved much of San Francisco from the ravages of nature and is equipped to save her from the ravages of man.

The hill's official name is Sutro Crest. Its popular name is Mount Sutro. It has been known as Blue Mountain and as Mount Parnassus.

The Crest is 918 feet above mean sea level, making it the city's third highest peak after Mount Davidson (936 feet) and the southern summit of the Twin Peaks (919 feet).

How did this hill save large sections of San Francisco?

That is partly the story of a man who lived silver - rich and died land - poor, Adolph Sutro. He tunneled into the Comstock Lode to make his silver fortune, but lost interest in the tunnel company when his partners squeezed him out of active management.

Sutro wrote in 1894:

"It was then, after they took the management away from me, that I sold out my stock in the concern quietly without its being known to anyone.

"I took my money and invested in real estate when . . . everybody was scared and thought the city was going to the dogs.

"I bought every acre I could lay my hands on until I had 2200 acres in this city."

Sutro's first land purchase here was 1400 acres of San Miguel Ranch south of Golden Gate Park. He changed the name of the ranch's highest point from Blue Mountain to Mt. Parnassus. But it became known popularly, even then, as Mount Sutro.

Nearly all the land Mr. Sutro bought here was sandy waste. They were uninhabited acres,

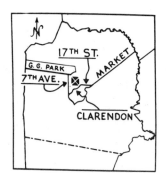

X marks Mt. Sutro

for the most part, that stretched to the Pacific. Strong southerly and westerly winds swirled the sand into dunes.

The man who had been called a fool when he began his Comstock Lode tunnel was called a fool again when he began buying the waste land.

On the southern slope of Mount Sutro, near the present location of the Sutro Forest Golf School and Driving Range at 1000 Clarendon avenue, Sutro set up a nursery.

There he tested plant after plant to determine which would hold the swirling sands onto his land, which amounted to about one - tenth of the city's area.

Mount Sutro's soil demonstrated the value of special bent and wire grasses imported from Europe. The soil of the slope also proved the holding power of eucalyptus, ash, pine and cypress trees.

Sutro planted with enthusiasm. He spread his bent and wire grasses over his lands in the Richmond and Sunset districts to keep the soil from blowing away. He planted hundreds of eucalypti over Mount Sutro and adjacent areas.

His heirs here say Sutro's plans were cut short by his death in 1898.

The southern slope of Mount Sutro (center) has been denuded of trees, bulldozed and terraced for a new housing project. The University of California owns the wooded northern slope, and the Government has leased four acres on the crest for a Nike missile site.

They say Sutro planted the eucalypti on Mount Sutro as a fast-growing shelter for smaller trees. His plans to tear out the eucalypti as soon as the ash and cypress began growing were dropped after his death.

The eucalypti grew and grew, smothering out the smaller trees. Mount Sutro and adjacent areas became almost impenetrable within thirty years after Sutro began planting in the 1880's. The area came to be called Sutro Forest.

Appraising Sutro's estate in 1910, A. S. Baldwin valued Mount Sutro and the Forest at $1800 an acre, and added: "This is one of the most picturesque tracts of land in San Francisco."

One of Sutro's daughters, Rosa B. Morbio, inherited ninety acres of Sutro Forest between Parnassus and Clarendon avenues.

Another ninety-acre Forest tract, including the southern slope of Mount Sutro, was inherited by another of Sutro's daughters, Clare de Choiseul, who subsequently willed the land to the Little Sisters of the Poor. Trees now have been uprooted from these slopes by residential developers.

Mrs. Morbio's ninety-acre tract was sold in 1947 to the University of California, which plans to use part of the land for Medical Center student housing.

The university in 1954 leased four acres on the peak of Mount Sutro to the United States. The lease, for $2000 a year, runs until 1964 and can be renewed.

There, on the top of the hill that produced plants to save much of San Francisco from nature, a dozen men attached to B Battery of the 740th AAA Missile Battalion operate radar and electronic control devices that might some day guide Nikes to enemy aircraft.

Mount Davidson and the Cross

Mt. Davidson's cross.

FIFTY MILES AT SEA, when the weather is right, travelers bound for San Francisco can see the Great Cross atop Mount Davidson. It is a mammoth structure, originally intended to be 100 feet in height. As it turned out, some concrete was left over, and thus the cross rises 103 feet above its massive base.

Mount Davidson itself, with an elevation of 938 feet, is the highest point in San Francisco. But despite its height, the mountain, which lies southwest of Twin Peaks, offers visitors almost no view of the city. All but its eastern edge is hemmed in by eucalyptus and pine trees, which block out virtually everything but the sky, the cross and the reddish soil sprinkled with golden poppies and forget-me-nots.

This was not always the case. When the mount was first surveyed in 1852 by George Davidson, it was unplanted. And Davidson, a pioneer government surveyor who mapped the Pacific Coast from San Diego to Puget Sound, named the peak Blue Mountain.

Adolph Sutro started planting trees on the peak with the aid of the city's school children in the early 1880's. By 1911, when the saplings had become trees, the hill was renamed in favor of Davidson.

The ceremony changing the name was attended by one man. Officials of the Sierra Club announced that the program would be delayed because of a storm. But Dr. Alexander G. McAdie, chief of the United States Weather Bureau in San Francisco from 1895 to 1913, declared: "Postpone it if you wish, but I will be there." Standing alone, he delivered his address to the wind and the rain and proclaimed the new name Mount Davidson.

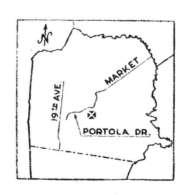

Where Mt. Davidson is.

The first of five crosses, a wooden symbol forty feet high, was erected in 1923 at the inspiration of James G. Decatur, telegraph official, YMCA director and prominent Episcopalian. In that year, worshipers climbed the mountain's woody trails for the first of the thirty-six annual Easter sunrise services that have been held there so far.

The cross was replaced the following year with a new one, eighty-seven feet high. But in 1928, vandals soaked its base in kerosene and set off a spectacular blaze. Another wooden cross was set afire in 1932. The fourth wooden cross, fifty feet in height, was erected temporarily (it soon fell down) while the permanent one was being shaped in concrete.

The present cross was completed in 1934, and it was first lighted when President Franklin D. Roosevelt pressed a gold telegraph key in the White House.

The cross contains 750 cubic yards of concrete, with a foundation sinking sixteen feet into bedrock. Its arms are nine feet square and measure thirty-nine feet across.

In a crypt at its base are buried such assorted things as stones from the Garden of Gethsemane, telephone books, Bibles, a jug of water from the River Jordan and copies of 1934 San Francisco newspapers. The water, incidentally, was kept in a vault of the American Trust Company during the construction period.

Except on Easter morning, the summit of Mount Davidson is an almost unpeopled place. The creaking of the eucalyptus trees is the loudest sound. The sound and sight of the city are almost forgotten.

Here is a view of Mt. Davidson looking south from Twin Peaks. At the far left are Glen Canyon and O'Shaughnessy boulevard. In the left center can be seen the contoured rows of houses that mark the Miraloma District. The eucalyptus covered summit of the city's highest hill in the center of the picture.

A Ridge Overlooked By History

NEAR THE southwest corner of San Francisco, rising 500 feet to a magnificent view from ocean to bay, is a ridge with three peaks.

The peaks are located, east to west, at Summit and Thrift streets; Shields street and Oriza-ba avenue, and Ramsell street near Shields.

Many names have been given to the hills — perhaps because no one cared about the ridge during the city's early years and no one lived there to perpetuate a name.

An old-time resident thinks it once was called Columbia Heights, but today that is a name adopted by an area on the southern side of the ridge.

Senior City Planner Elwood Gill recalls that about forty years ago it was "Lakeview Ridge."

In 1890 Adolph Sutro filed a map with the City Engineer of a proposed development on the eastern slope. He called it "Lakeview."

But maps in the City Engineer's office supply no name for the ridge nor the hills upon it.

Even today, most residents reply with a shrug when asked the name of the ridge upon which they live.

Those who suggest a name usually propose Merced Heights for the western half of the ridge and Ocean View for the eastern portion.

This is supported by James Keilty, who has done careful neighborhood studies for the City Planning Department. He too says: Merced Heights and Ocean View.

Although the ridge has virtually no formal history, a good guess can be made as to how the two names were conceived.

The western portion of the ridge overlooks Lake Merced.

At the foot of the eastern hill, near San Jose avenue, there once was a railroad station named Ocean View.

The ridge was the southern boundary of the Rancho San Miguel that comprised the heart of old San Francisco.

Cross marks
Merced Heights.

By 1867 it had caught the eyes of real estate developers who planned streets and filed maps with the City Engineer.

Ocean View was the project of the Railroad Homestead Association in 1867, and Merced Heights was the dream of the City Land Association in 1870.

However, despite the hopes of promoters, no one seems to have built upon the steep hillsides until after the earthquake and fire of 1906.

Among the first houses built were two on the northeast outcropping of the ridge, at the end of Harold street. Harold street was, and is, a winding pathway up the ridge.

Houses have now been built almost to the top of the eastern hill, which remains a barren peak of wind-swept rock.

Robert Browne, who has lived all his forty-seven years at 358 Howth street, recalls that in his youth there were only two small water tanks on the hill.

"When the wind was blowing the wrong way," Browne recalls, "we got the odor from the Chinese vegetable gardens near San Jose and Ocean avenues. They used shrimp and fish for fertilizer.

"There was nothing on the other hill (Merced Heights) except flowers. It was loaded down with pansies and we'd go over there to pick them. I remember people called it Pansy Hill."

To Merced Heights, following World War II, came builders who constructed single family homes with fine views.

In contrast to the naked granite of the eastern peaks, the western hilltop is crowned by a house and gardens and trees. The thriving vegetation represents half a lifetime of work by one woman.

Here, above the Jose Ortega Home School, live Helen Brooks and her husband, Jesse, owner of a stationery store.

Mrs. Brooks carted soil from the lowlands

The granite peak in the foreground marks the start of Merced Heights, which stretches west- **ward toward Lake Merced. It was once called Pansy Hill for the wild flowers growing there.**

and planted trees and grass on the unhospitable piece of rock. For twenty - two years she worked until today her hilltop is covered with greenery.

"The hill has changed a lot since we moved here," Mrs. Brooks said. "Somehow, it seems to me anyway, the wind doesn't blow as hard as it used to."

Where the Presidio Is Sublimest

The panorama that excited early Spanish explorers now includes the dome of the Palace of Fine Arts, the buildings on Alcatraz and the Presidio post buildings at the far right.

FATHER PEDRO FONT, journeying north with Lieutenant Colonel Juan Bautista de Anza, made this notation in his diary on March 28, 1776:

"We ascended a small, low hill, and then entered a tableland, entirely clear, of considerable extent, and flat, with a slight slope toward the port."

He probably was referring to the rise, now cypress-covered, known as Presidio Hill, the highest point on the military reservation De Anza ordered established here for Charles III of Spain before the opening shots of the American Revolutionary War had been fired.

Presidio Hill (elevation 370 feet) is just

inside the Arguello boulevard entrance to the Presidio of San Francisco. Hardly a musket-shot away, across a small valley, is another hill with a similar name, 309-foot Presidio Heights.

Just as Presidio Heights — that portion of the ridge generally described as Pacific Heights which overlooks the Presidio — is given over largely to impressive homes and apartment houses, Presidio Hill is devoted largely to recreation.

Built out from Arguello boulevard inside the Presidio on one slope of the hill is Inspiration Point, where view-wise San Franciscans can park their cars and look over the Palace of Fine Arts in the Marina toward Alcatraz and the hills of Marin county.

Another slope of the tree-topped hill is covered with the gently rolling fairways of the Presidio Golf Course.

In the valley between Presidio Hill and Presidio Heights are the tennis courts, basketball nets and soccer field of Julius Kahn Playground, covering six acres of land within the Presidio and operated by the City Park and Recreation Department under a Federal license granted in 1922.

The playground faces Pacific avenue, here a one-way street at the base of Pacific Heights, and is overlooked by the well-kept homes of San Franciscans whose names would be included in any who's-who listing of local socialites.

Presidio Hill overlooks a military reservation which, after a bad-to-worse beginning, has become one of the Nation's most beautiful and most valuable.

Laid out by De Anza in March, 1776, the Presidio was established

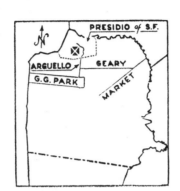

X marks Presidio Hill.

in September of the same year by Lieutenant Jose Joaquin Moraga. The house built for Moraga on the Presidio near the base of Presidio Hill, still stands. Greatly remodeled, this oldest building in San Francisco now is the Presidio Officers Club.

The Presidio church and many of the buildings constructed under Moraga's command were destroyed in the 1812 earthquake. The Spaniards hardly had rebuilt the Presidio when the Mexicans revolted in 1821 and took over the fortification.

Mexico let the Presidio go to pot. Regular troops were withdrawn in 1835, leaving a single soldier as caretaker, and the Presidio walls and buildings crumbled into decay.

The United States took over the installation after Commander John B. Montgomery raised the Stars and Stripes over San Francisco in 1846.

In 1898, some 30,000 men were organized, equipped and trained in the shadow of Presidio Hill to fight in the Spanish-American War.

A tent city rose on the slopes of the hill in 1906 when the area filled with refugees from the great fire and earthquake.

As late as 1911, the Presidio was still an old-time Army fort that clung to kerosene lamps and mildewed walls. But Congress that year appropriated $6,000,000 to make the Presidio the greatest fort in the West.

Among the improvements: A six-million-gallon reservoir built on the crest of Presidio Hill to supply the fortification's fresh water needs.

Enemy aliens were housed at the Presidio during World War I, and top brass of the Western Defense Command were there during World War II. The Presidio now is headquarters of the Sixth Army.

The old Presidio wall is in a vale dividing Presidio Hill from Presidio Heights. It also divides two ways of life: military and social.

A Steep, Green Country Hill

ONE OF San Francisco's most attractive little hills — northwest of Portola drive between Forest Hill and Mount Davidson — has no name of its own.

"Edgehill Heights," the city's departments call it, though it is neither a bluff nor on the edge of anything, but an abrupt and independent little hill rising to about 600 feet. The name was taken from its single street, Edgehill way, which winds up to encircle its summit.

The United States Geological Survey and old city maps show it only as one of the San Miguel hills, of which 938 - foot Mount Davidson is the chief. They were so named because they lay mostly within the old San Miguel Rancho before San Francisco grew southward and the land was subdivided.

But, name or no name, the little hill has a delightfully countrified atmosphere, a quiet greenness rare in the city.

The effect, enthusiastically guarded by the residents of the twenty - odd homes there, is largely a result of its steepness. Many lots have never been built on because they are so nearly vertical, and over the years they have become heavily wooded with cypress and pine. Backyards, too, are often tree - filled, because only a goat could garden them.

The houses look out over expansive views of the city, the uppermost sweeping immense vistas from Twin Peaks to Westlake, from Mount Davidson to all the hazy ranges of hills east of the Bay.

The owners maintain Edgehill way themselves through an association, since it was built without the storm sewer system and other refinements that the city requires before it will maintain a street.

From Portola drive motorists identify the hill by the huge scar carved into its side by excavation. This led to the only news the hill has made — a legal dispute when one of its houses above the excavation started to slide in the rains of early 1952.

Now from Portola drive the passerby can see the extensive concrete foundation that was required to prop the house and the part of Edgehill way that had been damaged by the slide.

Again last winter the street was damaged above the excavation, and the owners of the property below were notified by the city that they must see to its repair. Until that is completed visitors cannot, as formerly, drive around the hilltop for a survey of its magnificent vistas.

Although little known, the hill was one of the first real subdivisions in the city. Parkside is said to have been the first, followed by Forest Hill, St. Francis Wood, West Portal Park and then the Edgehill way area which was called Claremont Court — a name that has disappeared today except on the Assessor's map.

Edgehill way was first listed in the city directory in 1922.

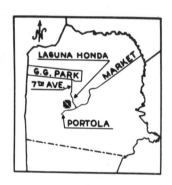

X marks Edgehill.

Edgehill Way's tree-covered 600-foot-high hill as it appears from a rooftop of the Laguna Honda Home for the Aged. The camera is facing somewhat west of south.

Looking northwest from Edgehill Way one can see the Marin county hills in the distance.

City Surrounded, But Didn't Top This Hill

THE TOP of Bernal Heights is as unashamedly rural as the outskirts of Petaluma — but a few blocks below are four of San Francisco's busiest thoroughfares.

To the east of the 325-foot-high hill is Bayshore Freeway and to the west is Mission street. Army street forms the northern boundary and Alemany boulevard the southern.

But above the traffic noise a family of skunks has found refuge from the neighborhood dogs in a snug home of blackberry brambles.

And toward the summit Bonview street trails off into a dirt road against a fantastic backdrop of the distant bay and the ant-like activity of the millions who crowd its shores.

Bernal Heights disdained urbanity even in its past. It is one of the few metropolitan areas which can claim to have had both a gold rush and a range war.

The gold rush was short lived. The fever broke out in May of 1876 when a Frenchman named Victor Resayre announced the discovery of ore on the summit which he said would assay at $1,000,000 a ton.

A lot of rock was crushed on Bernal Heights in the day or so it took to learn that a ton of it wouldn't buy a one-way ride on a horse car.

The range war was small in scope, but intense. On one side were the city poundmen who made their sole living by the fees they received for the return or sale of impounded animals.

On the other side were the Irish who settled the hill when it was subdivided in the

Cross marks Bernal Heights.

decade after the Civil War. Most of the settlers kept a cow or a couple of goats. Often the animals would disappear, and the poundmen were blamed.

One day the Widow O'Brien's cow was taken. This was too much. The lady, who had reared two daughters by her own hard work, was the most respected person on the heights.

Every man, boy and dog on the hill assembled and roughed up the poundmen and drove them off the heights. The interlopers never returned.

After the 1906 earthquake and fire a second wave of settlers built homes on the hill. Lumber was provided for those who would purchase a lot for resettlement. Many of these "emergency" houses still stand today.

Margaret Prestidge of 56 Bonview street lives in such a house built by her father. She was born there and watched the city comforts of paved roads and bus service creep up the hill, but never quite reach the top.

She said that the area around her has retained the close-knit friendliness of a country town. Everybody knows everybody else — and the children and dogs thrive.

As for the weather, Mrs. Prestidge said there is little fog, but the winds could be slowed down a bit without anyone's complaining.

The top of the hill is covered by city-owned land that may become a park one day. A drive around Bernal Heights boulevard, which circles the top, provides a clear impression of this pastoral island which rises unexpectedly above a giant city.

Bernal Heights dominates the central horizon and reaches cloudward. Rows of houses climb only part way up its southern slope. To the right the Freeway curves, leading downtown.

Rural Bernal Heights — the shingle house was one of the do-it-yourself homesteads built by refugees from 1906 earthquake.

A Home on Mount St. Joseph's

On top of Mount St. Joseph's stands a Catholic orphange.   The brick building serves as a home

ON AUGUST 18, 1852, a small group of Catholic Sisters of Charity arrived in San Francisco.

They came from Emmitsburg, Maryland, at the request of Archbishop Joseph Alemany, to set up an orphanage here.

It was a long trip by sea to the Isthmus of Panama, by pack train to the Pacific, and then up the coast. Several were stricken with cholera.

They established their orphanage at the corner of Market and Montgomery streets. But soon the quarters were too small, and the director, Sister Frances Assisium McEnnis, went looking for new quarters.

In 1861 she wrote: "I have purchased a very nice piece of ground in the country just four miles from the city on the San Bruno road (now Third street). There are forty-seven acres, a small house and a fine orchard . . ."

The new orphanage, named Mount St. Joseph's by the Sisters, was completed in 1869 and children were moved in. The big four-story frame building survived the 1906 earthquake, but disaster struck in 1910 and the orphanage was leveled by fire.

A new brick building was built atop the 250-foot hill in 1911. It stands today as a home for one hundred and sixty-two girls between the ages of five and eighteen years.

Of the original forty-seven acres, fifteen remain as property belonging to the orphanage. The main building faces Newhall street, overlooking Hunters Point Naval Shipyard and the Bayview District.

Bridgeview drive winds around the north-

for 162 girls. At right, All Hallows Church, to the left, Bayview Grammar School.

ern border of the property from Newhall street to Topeka avenue on the southwest.

Other than the structure itself, little is the same as it was in 1911.

Now the orphans live in seven separate "apartments," separated by age groups. Each apartment is divided into several rooms, all brightly painted and modestly but attractively furnished.

Three or four girls share a bedroom and dine with other girls from their apartments. Among the teen-agers radios blare, phonograph records spin, and the talk is just like the talk of other girls the same age.

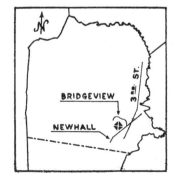

Cross marks
"The Mount"

"It's the modern idea," said Sister Mary Daniel, now director of the orphanage. "We know these children need love and care, but they also need as much privacy as possible.

A Sister is group mother for each apartment, living and eating with her children, sharing their problems and helping them.

To widen the social relationships and make possible greater community contacts, girls from the third through twelfth grades attend several different grade and high schools. Older girls may attend school dances or invite their friends to "The Mount" for dinner or week ends.

Summit With a Future

The barren, table-topped peak known as Gold Mine Hill lies just southeast of Twin Peaks.

Part of the Crocker estate for seventy years, it is now part of the Diamond Heights Project.

Cross marks the hill.

So FAR AS ANYONE KNOWS, there was never a gold mine on Gold Mine Hill. But the glamor of its past is no less fascinating for the lack of a few tons of gold.

It is a barren peak, rising 679 feet above sea level — one of the highest hills in the city — overlooking Glen Canyon and Glen Park on the one side, and Thirtieth and Douglass streets on the other.

Fred Schlichting, chief land agent for the City's Redevelopment Agency, says the Gold Mine name ap-

Russian smugglers used the hill to hide their goods. And, legend has it that at least one group was hanged on the hill.

pears on all the maps he has found of the hill. But it might better have been called Russian Smugglers' Hill.

Schlichting, in his investigations into ownership of land for the Diamond Heights Redevelopment Project, met an old man who passed on the story of the smugglers.

The man said his grandfather, who had a cabin in the area, told him about the Russian smugglers who had a cave somewhere in Glen Canyon, on the southern slope.

They would come ashore off what is now Ocean Beach and move their goods inland as far as Gold Mine Hill, hiding out there until they could smuggle them on into San Francisco.

And it was on that hill, the old man told Schlichting, that at least one group of smugglers was hanged.

Gold Mine Hill was part of the San Miguel Rancho, but its steep slopes and rocky outcroppings made it of little value, even for grazing land.

The Crocker Estate Company, formed at the death of Charles Crocker to administer his holdings for the heirs, bought the 166-acre site in 1889.

Portions of the acreage were sold through the years, including a large plot to the city for the Glen Park Playground.

But the topmost twenty-one acres remain in the Crocker Estate — these acres stretching across the rocky peak where, during World War II, an anti-aircraft gun emplacement kept guard over the city.

The hill now seems to serve no better purpose than as as wind-break for the houses and apartments on the eastern slope.

It is under condemnation as part of the Diamond Heights Project and will, for the first time in recorded city history, pass from the hands of the Crocker family.

But with the passing goes an opportunity for knowledgeable squatters to find a free homesite — at least temporarily.

City records show that the Crocker Company has never re-established its proof of ownership on the land since titles were destroyed in the 1906 fire. Because no one ever challenged Crocker and because Crocker apparently paid the taxes when they became due, the issue has never come up.

But if someone had tried to claim the land — or simply to move onto it — the owners would have faced a bothersome court fight to remove them; and it might have proved cheaper just to give the squatter the land he was on.

But it's too late for that experiment now. The future of Gold Mine Hill is secure in the hands of the Redevelopment Agency.

Holly Park Hill-Low But Pleasantly Green

FOR SHEER HEIGHT, Holly Park Hill would make more of a mark gracing the flatlands of Lincoln, Nebraska, than it does in stridently vertical San Francisco.

But the hill's easy rise (it's only 274 feet above sea level and is dwarfed by neighboring Bernal Heights) makes it a fine place for children to play. A lost ball can be recaptured before it rolls into the street.

The limits of Holly Park Hill are the limits of the park itself. Both are neatly enclosed by an oval street named, with a certain disregard for geometry, "Holly Park Circle."

The hill is two blocks east of Mission street on Highland avenue. That means the park, compact in size, is in the center of a densely populated area. Yet it is pleasantly uncrowded.

A grove of eucalyptus, cypress and Monterey pine trees stands on the southern part of the hill and serves as a windbreak. The green mound holds swings and other apparatus for the smaller children, and there is plenty of room to play softball.

Funds to improve Holly Park's playground facilities were voted in the 1955 bond issue. Work on the $100,000 project, however, will not begin until next year.

The land on which Holly Park stands was deeded to the city in 1860 by Harvey S. Brown and John F. Cobb, but not accepted by the Board of Supervisors until ten years later.

Brown was one of the leading attorneys for Southern Pacific Railroad, serving with it thirty years before his retirement in 1893 at the age of 70. He came to San Francisco in 1849 from his home town of Matsonville, N.Y. He died in Oakland in 1911.

The city reservoir which adjoins the park to the northwest was constructed in 1870. It was then known as George's Hill Reservoir, but subsequently was renamed "College

Cross marks Holly Park Hill.

Hill," in honor of nearby St. Mary's College.

St. Mary's College, the tall gothic spires of which once rose two blocks south of Holly Park, has since moved to the East Bay.

The cornerstone of the college was laid in 1862 by the Rt. Rev. Joseph Sadoc Alemany, first Catholic Archbishop of San Francisco, after whom Alemany boulevard was named.

The college stayed in San Francisco until 1889, when pressure for space in the rapidly growing area became intolerable. The school, a men's liberal arts institution, is now in Moraga Valley, Contra Costa county.

Holly Court Housing Project, west of the park, was the first Federal low-cost housing to be built on the Pacific Coast. It was completed May 1, 1940, at a cost of $558,000 for its 118 units.

According to the San Francisco Housing Authority, Holly Court is still the most popular project in the city for applicants and has the lowest turnover.

Across the street from the park is Junipero Serra Elementary School, built in 1911. During the school year children swarm across the green hill.

That's Holly Park Hill — a lucky bit of elbow room and a momentary relief from concrete and steel.

The gentle rise of Holly Park Hill stands out like an island of green in the midst of a sea of concrete, wood and steel in this view, looking south from Bernal Heights.

Well-known characters of old San Francisco, from an 1854 caricature.

Twin Peaks: Boss View of Them All

From Twin Peaks the city opens like a book, with Market street the binding line. To the left you can see the towers of the financial district.

To the right, the South of Market area and the eight-mile-long Bay Bridge. Beyond, in the distance, are the East Bay's hills.

THE TWIN PEAKS, says an Indian legend, were once a single mountain — man and wife. But the couple quarreled long and bitterly until finally the Great Spirit split them apart with a bolt of lightning. The neighborhood has been quiet ever since.

The Spaniards had a more sentimental view of the hills. They called the peaks "*Los Pechos de la Choca*," or "The Breasts of the Indian Maiden," in memory of a tall, slender and softly beautiful girl. N. P. Vallejo, son of the famed General Mariano Vallejo, reminisced years later about the maid: "Never have I seen a cultured woman half so fair as this untaught, uninstructed daughter of the wilds."

Now the maiden has some jewelry, of sorts — a reservoir, a split roadway making a figure 8 around the peaks and two new police radio towers. A geodetic marker is planted at the top of the

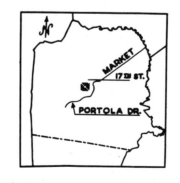

X marks Twin Peaks.

South Peak (elevation 910 feet), and a similar marker has vanished from the top of North Peak (elevation 903 feet). The two and one-half mile Twin Peaks Tunnel carries street cars far below the wild, windy surface, and real estate subdivisions are crawling up the slopes.

The reservoir has been there since 1912, and it was opened with a grand round of ceremonies. One hundred American Flags were planted around the rim. Every politician with air in his lungs was allowed to speak. There were songs in between and bands played martial airs. Marathon racers panted up from the Noe and Eureka valleys.

Then, late in the afternoon, all San Francisco was invited to dance inside the empty reservoir. When the dancers left, the tank was filled.

Three years later, the city declared the peaks a public park. The fifteen - acre core of the park

A split roadway makes a perfect figure eight around the Twin Peaks.

(which later grew to sixty-five acres) cost $13,740.

The tunnel opened in 1917, and civilization began appearing on the hillside. Twin Peaks boulevard was built and then paved.

But the peaks remain a wild place. The soil is red and rocky. It supports only grass and some wild flowers, chiefly poppies. The wind roars by, cold and harsh — so cold a visitor's ears hurt if he stands too long at the summit of one of the mounds.

And the peaks still serve well as guardians of what once were the pasture lands of the Mission, blocking the cold sea wind and fog.

Most importantly for most San Franciscans and visitors, they command the finest view in town — the ocean, the Golden Gate, the Bay, Mounts Tamalpais and Diablo and the city itself.

There are views in all directions, but the prize of them all is to the east, with Market street splitting the scene in half. The Ferry

Building is straight ahead. To the left, going down Market, are the U. S. Mint and the tall downtown office buildings. Farther left, City Hall and the Opera House dominate the Civic Center. Still farther left are the apartment houses of Nob Hill and Russian Hill, with Coit Tower and the tip of Telegraph Hill peeking between. And sweeping even farther left, behind the new radio tower, are the apartment houses and the mansions of Pacific Heights.

To the right, the Merchandise Mart looms on the south side of Market street. Farther downtown, the Telegraph Building on New Montgomery street stands alone. The Bay Bridge stretches across to Yerba Buena Island and the East Bay, with freeways stretching back toward the Peninsula. The domed National Guard Armory at Fourteenth and Mission streets and Everett Junior High School and Sanchez Elementary School are in the foreground.

Excelsior Heights Settlers Stay On

FOR THE STORY of Excelsior Heights, a remarkably unchanging little island in San Francisco's ever-moving sea of people, go to men like Joe Delorio, a bakery driver, or his father, Louis, a retired boilermaker.

Excelsior Heights (elevation 315 feet) manages to dominate the whole broad Excelsior District south of Mission between Silver and Geneva avenues, but files of the California Historical Society show not a single reference to the hill or the district.

"I think we'll have to credit Henry Wadsworth Longfellow with the name," said James Keilty of the City Planning Department. "At one time there were Excelsior districts in practically every city in the United States. Remember Longfellow's poem? 'A banner with the strange device, Excelsior!'"

The word means "ever upward," a grandiose label for a 315-foot hill. The "ever" part of the definition still fits very well, however, Associate Planner Keilty reports.

"It's surprising how many long-time residents are still in that neighborhood," he said. "I talked to a woman the other day who lives just two blocks from the house where she was born . . ."

Joe Delorio is one of that unchanging group of long-time residents. His home at 700 Edinburgh is less than two blocks from that of his parents at 730 Madrid street.

"I'm 43 now, and I was only two years old when the folks moved here from North Beach," the son explained.

"There have been only two big changes — instead of muddy roads, we now have paved streets and sidewalks, and there are a great many more houses here now."

The growth has been slow and steady as well as durable, he said — no sudden boom at any one time. The attraction must be the people who live there or, in some cases, the view, because not even Delorio claims the best climate in town.

"I think we're in a little fog belt out here," he confided. "It's not as sunny as the old Mission District farther north."

There's the attraction of parks and playgrounds, however — big John McLaren Park, the adjacent Crocker-Amazon Playground on the north slope of the hill itself.

"Crocker-Amazon was made into a Navy housing project during the war, but they've torn out those shacks now and it'll be a recreational area again," Delorio said.

"I can remember years ago when everybody called it 'The Dago Gardens,' and it had nine baseball diamonds."

The Excelsior District has long been one of the centers of Italian-American population in San Francisco, Planner Keilty said, although the neighborhood today includes many Irish, Anglo-Saxon, Central European and Latin-American names.

The streets fit in this pleasantly mixed pattern perfectly; streets like London, Paris, Lisbon, Madrid, Naples, Edinburgh, Vienna, Munich, Athens, Moscow, Prague and Dublin cross such avenues as France, Russia, Persia and Brazil. For some odd reason, two capitals — Rome and Berlin — were ignored when the streets were named. Instead there are Naples and Munich.

There's also an Excelsior avenue, of course, a long block north of Brazil.

And across Mission street to the north, the branch postoffice on Onondaga avenue is labeled in big letters: Excelsior Station.

It's no longer carried on Federal books that way, however, The Chronicle learned.

Asked how Excelsior Station got its name, Postmaster John F. Fixa's office reported: "Excelsior? We don't have any Excelsior station . . . Oh, the one on Onondaga? You mean Station F."

The Delorios and their neighbors don't mind. Excelsior is still Excelsior, and its residents seem determined to stay forever.

This view of the hill is from the top of the Pacific Telephone building on Onondaga ave-nue. The buildings in the foreground front on Mission street. Russia street is at the left.

Cross marks
Excelsior Heights

A Soaring Future for Red Rock Hill

R ED ROCK HILL is a spectacular bit of nothing much with a highly enterprising future. The hill's current inventory includes acres of disheartened grass and an outcropping of rock which does manage to look red in the proper light.

But the word spectacular is apt because the hill is high — 689 feet above sea level — and commands any number of distant views from its summit due south of Clipper street in the Diamond Heights area.

Red Rock Hill is one of the Diamond Heights itself (the other two being Gold Mine and Fairmount hills to the southeast). And that's why the future is the main thing about the hill. The rocks are going to be leveled for tower apartment sites as part of the Diamond Heights Redevelopment Program.

This future began in the past — 1905 to be exact — when an architect and city planner named Daniel H. Burnham came to San Francisco to see what needed to be done.

The city planner settled on Twin Peaks, which is in frowning distance of Red Rock Hill. The reason Burnham frowned was because the hill was bare, although it had been subdivided and resubdivided since the Civil War.

There was even a nice grid pattern of streets running to the top of Red Rock Hill — but the streets were on paper only. Burnham set about and re-planned the three hills of Diamond Heights, designing contour streets which co-operated with, rather than challenged, the terrain.

This new design was recommended to San Francisco in the Burnham report of 1905. But before the matter could be given much thought, Nature came up with some gratuitous city planning of its own in the earthquake and fire of 1906. Burnham's less drastic plans for Diamonds Heights were ignored in the hurried rebuilding that ensued.

Meanwhile, quarrying continued and cows grazed on the hillside. (A dairy existed in a nearby canyon until the early 1930's.) But this bucolic atmosphere could not withstand San Francisco's post World War II population boom. By July, 1950,

No. 1 on this model shows plans for Red Rock Hill in the Diamond Heights Redevelopment Program, soon to be built.

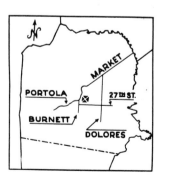

X marks Red Rock Hill.

Diamond Heights was designated a redevelopment area by the Board of Supervisors.

This action was taken under a law which provides that government funds will be used for clearing and preparing the land and setting up

Red Rock Hill (central horizon) is fated for private homes and three ten-story apartment buildings. Now the 689-foot hill is alone with its reddish rock, grass and wide vistas.

public facilities. The government then is to sell the land to private developers who agree to build in accordance with a central plan. These developers will own the property.

Thus far, the Redevelopment Agency has purchased seventy-five per cent of the land on Red Rock and its two neighboring hills. The agency is in litigation for the balance. All this takes time. The end result should be a new community of 7500 people with its own schools, churches, shops, etc.

Detached houses, row houses, garden courts and apartments will be built. The tallest buildings, including three ten-story apartments, will be erected on Red Rock Hill, since it is closest to downtown San Francisco.

A Scholarly Summit on Geary

Architectural scale model of George Washington High School on top of Washington Heights.

WASHINGTON HEIGHTS figures little in the early history of San Francisco. It simply rose a little higher than the sand dunes which then covered the area.

Nearby, on what was then the Point Lobos road and is now Geary boulevard, carriages and horse cars tracked to the Cliff House and back to San Francisco. The area around the hill was known as the "outside lands," remote and unimportant.

The men who quarried rock on Washington Heights back in the 1860's were out to make on honest dollar — they didn't know they were digging an athletic stadium.

But the hollow they left in the side of the Richmond District hill now is carpeted with carefully trimmed grass and lined with tiers of bleachers.

On the bleachers in good football weather are students from George Washington High School, which sits on top of the 260-foot hill and gives it its name. The school covers six-

Cross marks the hill

teen acres bounded by Geary boulevard, Balboa street and Thirtieth and Thirty-second avenues.

This year the students are dressed in a bobby sox and dirty saddle shoe uniform not noticeably different from that worn by the school's first graduating class in 1938.

The school achieved national recognition in the *Reader's Digest* last March in an article titled "Three Cheers for George Washington High!"

The area of the hill not occupied by the high school is mostly residential, white rows of houses built over garages shoulder to shoulder in familiar San Francisco pattern.

But at one address, 741 Thirtieth avenue, is a rambling, domestic-looking structure which houses a school as interesting in its way and as vitally important to some as the high school above it. This is the Lucinda Weeks School, for the physically, mentally and emotionally handicapped.

The Richmond District's Washington Heights rises 260 feet high on the horizon. Geary boulevard, running past the hill, was once the main carriage route to the Cliff House.

This photograph shows George Washington High School's first graduation exercises, 1938.

Mount Olympus: View From City's Center

The panoramic view from 570-foot Mount Olympus takes in Corona Heights on the right; Buena Vista Park directly ahead, and East Bay and Marin county hills in the background.

MOUNT OLYMPUS, although not one of San Francisco's best known hills, is easy to find on a map, for it is located right in the middle — at the city's geographical center.

And as such, the 570-foot bluff, topped by an empty monument pedestal, provides a particularly satisfying point from which to view the city's sprawling vista of bay, peaks, ocean, parks and bridges. On a clear day you can see ten counties.

Most authorities agree the hill was named after the ancient Greek gods' cloud-capped home. And the streets that wind up its slopes — Mars, Vulcan and Saturn — would seem to bear them out.

But there is a pleasant legend that hangs on: That a genial milk-peddler called Hanrahan was responsible for the name.

Hanrahan became known as "Old Limpus" as he delivered his wares during the 1860's at the base of the hill because of a crippled leg.

So, when it came time to name the peak, the story has it that residents decided to honor the hard-working milkman and call it "Mount Old Limpus." Through course of verbal usage, "Old Limpus" supposedly became "Olympus."

Until several years ago, the real sight of

the hill was a twelve - foot - high cast concrete copy of a much smaller statue by the Belgian artist Antoine Wiertz.

Titled "Triumph of Light," it showed a classically proportioned Goddess of Liberty — her arms outstretched and waving a torch — triumphing over a sinister winged demon, the fiend of darkness.

The statue was placed on its thirty - foot pedestal in 1887 by Adolph Sutro in pomp - filled dedication ceremonies punctuated by fiery oratory and patriotic song.

But the statue had a hard life. The goddess' right arm and torch were early snatched away — some say by irate sailors of the day

Cross marks Mt. Olympus

who found that her light threw them off their course as they maneuvered their ships through the Golden Gate.

The concrete weathered and crumbled. Water got to the statue's metal supports and four years ago the city decided to take it down as disreputable, and a hazard to boot.

So all that is left on the crest of Mount Olympus is a massive pedestal — its inscription defaced and illegible.

Mount Olympus is about where Sixteenth and Ashbury streets would intersect if the contour of the land permitted them to do so. It is reached by climbing Upper Terrace, which winds through the quiet residential district.

Famous Nob Hill---"The Best of San Francisco"

From the balcony of the new Masonic Auditorium on Nob Hill, this photographic panorama sweeps the city from the Marine's Memorial Building at the extreme left, past the

WHEN Robert Louis Stevenson came to San Francisco before the turn of the century, he surveyed Nob Hill and wrote:

"The great net of straight thoroughfares lying at right angles east and west and north and south over the shoulders of Nob Hill, the hill of palaces, must certainly be counted the best part of San Francisco.

"It is there that the millionaires who gathered together, vying with each other in display, looked down upon the business wards of the city."

Stevenson would find that the description still fits the hill today: the streets, from their gridiron pattern, still soar dizzily into the sky; the city's rich and power-

ful still overlook the commercial district, and though the palaces are gone, luxurious apartments have risen in their place.

The first known resident of Nob Hill was Dr. Arthur Hayne, a well-to-do dentist, who erected a wood and clay structure on the present site of the Fairmont Hotel in 1856.

Society followed his lead, leaving their stately old homes on Rincon Hill and South Park to build gaudy new mansions on California, Sacramento, Taylor and Mason streets.

The settlers included such names as William Walton, Lloyd Tevis, Senator George Hearst, Leland Stanford, Mark Hopkins, Charles Crocker, James C. Flood, James Fair and Collis P. Hunt-

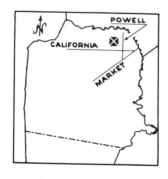

X locates Nob Hill.

dome of the City Hall (center), out to Lone Mountain at the far right of the picture.

ington. In the 1870's the California street cable car was established by Stanford to make access to his home easier.

Nobody knows for sure how the hill got its name. Life was fast and high on Nob Hill during the champagne days of the Nineties, then the earthquake and fire leveled the palaces.

But the hill was rebuilt — one of its tallest buildings, the Clay - Jones Apartments, stands kitty - corner from the summit of the hill, 376 feet, the highest of the downtown hills.

The great names still remain: Mark Hopkins Hotel, Fairmont Hotel, Stanford Apartments and Huntington Park.

The view is still overwhelming. Stand at California and Mason as the lively evening crowds sweep across the whirring cable slot and look out — past the golden necklace of the Bay Bridge, to the East Bay's jewel box of lights beyond.

The home of Mark Hopkins stood on the present site of the famous Mark Hopkins Hotel.

When St. Mary's College Was Part of San Francisco

THE BELLS OF ST. MARY'S haven't echoed across College Hill for many a year, and most of the residents today don't know how their little hilltop south of the Mission District got its name.

The 200-foot crest rises abruptly beside a steep cut — once a railroad right-of-way — through which San Jose avenue now carries heavy streams of auto traffic. Two streets, neither with direct access to San Jose avenue, serve the hilltop homes.

College avenue climbs northward from St. Mary's avenue to the hilltop, then turns eastward, skips across Mission street and curves back to the south — and still farther downhill — into a neat residential area that once was the site of St. Mary's College.

A cross-topped little monument in the center of divided College avenue labels this district St. Mary's Park. Adjoining it to the east and spreading irregularly over nearly a dozen blocks is St. Mary's Park Playground.

The second street serving College Hill is a small byway named College Terrace — which does not cross Mission into the St. Mary's Park area at all. Nevertheless, it was reportedly laid out to provide homesites for some of the college staff, Associate Planner James Keilty of the City Planning Department said.

Both the avenue and the terrace were un-doubtedly named College because of their nearness to St. Mary's College, Keilty reported.

No trace remains of the Gothic spires of the college itself, which was moved to the East Bay in 1889.

The cornerstone of the college, a liberal arts institution for men, was laid in 1862 by the Rt. Rev. Joseph Sadoc Alemany, first Catholic Archbishop of San Francisco, for whom Alemany boulevard was named.

By 1889, the college, unable to get the additional space it needed at its original location, was moved to Oakland, and then to the Moraga Valley in Contra Costa county in 1928.

A city reservoir site adjoining Holly Park, a few blocks north of St. Mary's Park, is sometimes described as College Hill and it is, in fact, part of the same ridge of high ground. But the only reference in files of the California Historical Society describe College Hill like this:

"Bounded by Mission street, St. Mary's avenue, the Southern Pacific right-of-way (now San Jose avenue) and Richland avenue."

And at least a decade ago, City Planning Department records had accepted that description.

The city at that time had compiled a list of the forty-four most prominent hilltops in San Francisco, and College Hill was on the list.

X marks College Hill.

This is College Hill (with its crest at far left). The spires of St. John's Church rise in the background.

Seventy years ago, the bells of old St. Mary's College were a familiar sound to residents of College Hill.

St. Mary's College looked much like this when it stood on College Hill from 1863 to 1889. The actual buildings differed slightly from this architect's sketch.

Historic Little Ridge On

Historic old Hunters Point Ridge rises in a gentle curve in the distance. Marching in ser- ried ranks across the slope are the San Francisco Housing Authority's 2723 units.

IN ALL OF SAN FRANCISCO, deep salt water and a good supply of fresh water were never found closer together than at Hunters Point — a fact which led indirectly to an agreement that the name of the point shall never be changed.

The good fresh water came from excellent springs on Hunters Point Ridge, a major landmark among the historic hills of San Francisco despite the fact it rises only 275 feet above the Bay.

Because the Bay was relatively deep close to shore, ships began going to the point more than a century ago to take on fresh water — and eventually subdividers and a ship repair company began to develop the area.

The first recorded exploration of the area by boat came in 1775, when a longboat of the vessel *San Carlos* landed Spanish explorers on the point. They called it Seashell Point, and the only settlers they encountered were a few Indians from villages in what are now Visitacion Valley and Brisbane.

By 1849, after ships of the pre-gold rush era had begun to use the point in increasing numbers, the subdividing firm of Townsend and DeBoom became active there. Among other arrivals at the time were several members of the Hunter family, who lived on the southeast slope of the hill.

In 1868, William C. Ralston, then a director of the California Steam Navigation Co., built a huge granite drydock on the point — and as part of the deal by which he acquired some of the Hunter property, he agreed that the name then in use — Hunters Point — should never be changed.

The United States Navy, which took over the shipyard in World War II, has honored the same agreement, whether it was bound by it or not. In Navy records, the installation remains "San Francisco Naval Shipyard at Hunters Point."

Ralston's drydock, cut almost entirely from solid rock, was 465 feet long and 120 feet wide, and cost an astonishing $1,200,000 despite the low prices and low wages of the era. Additional granite blocks were needed and were hauled laboriously by ox team from the Rocklin quarries in the Sacramento Valley.

Hunters Point

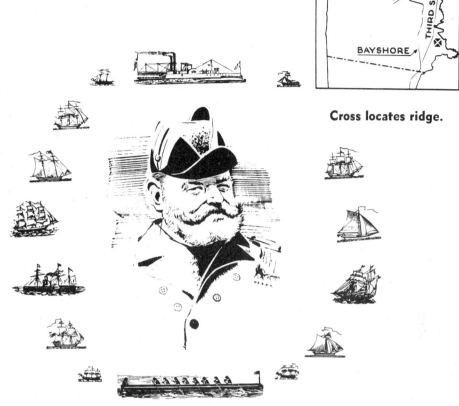

Cross locates ridge.

The dock remained in use until 1916, when a 1020-foot graving dock replaced it.

There were never many buildings of any kind atop the ridge, although a few houses and a church were built there.

On the south slope, one of the earliest Italian gardens in the area was started before 1860 by the Finocchio family; and within another decade, the Chinese shrimp industry was beginning to make the point a headquarters.

An Italian contributed indirectly to that industry, too, historians of the time reported. A jobless Chinese cook begged food, got a few shrimp from an Italian fisherman, and realized the commercial possibilities.

On the ridge itself, from Hilltop road to East Point road, all but a few of the buildings are now publicly owned. The San Francisco Housing Authority, which took over temporary war-time housing and subsequently has been replacing it with permanent units, now has a total of 2723 units at Hunters Point.

Two privately owned buildings remain. One houses a grocery store, beauty shop and cleaning establishment. The other is a church.

There are also five school buildings owned by the San Francisco School District, a large gym leased by the Housing Authority for $1 a year from the Recreation and Park Department, and a new $250,000 community building now under construction.

"The ridge was pretty much vacant before the war," said John W. Beard, executive director of the Housing Authority. But the Authority inherited a total of 10,000 units of temporary war housing after the war ended — the last of them due to be razed by 1962.

Many already have been replaced, but 1830 (known as Ridge Point) are still in use on and around the hill, along with these newer permanent projects:

Hunters Point, on the south slope and adjoining the naval reservation, 317 units in use and another 100 under construction; Harbor Slope, on the north slope, 226 apartments, and Hunters View, on another knoll to the west and north, with 350 apartments.

So far as Beard can tell, the ridge never will be vacant again.

"We have long waiting lists for all of our units," he said.

A City Hill That Man Has Cut Away

THE FABLED HILLS of San Francisco have been limned on these pages; their past glories told, their vistas pictured, and their contemporary life explored.

Our chronicle of the city's hills ends with a hill that is gone forever.

Once it was part of the San Francisco pageant, a high eminence overlooking the Bay and crowded with the roistering young buckos who helped to build the metropolis.

Now it is only a memory, a shorn, bald patch of rock and weed that has been scraped and blasted and graded and leveled.

It is called Irish Hill.

You'd never find it unless you were an intimate.

Forty - two hills ago The Chronicle began this story to keep alive the legends of San Francisco's up-and-down geography.

Today it is unlikely that any reader of these pages would persist in believing that, as some guide books say, San Francisco has seven hills. Seven is an aping of Rome, and San Francisco never apes.

But just how many hills there are has never been quite clear. This series, now that it is over, counts forty - two. Based on historical records, contour maps, and musty records at City Hall, the number forty - two seems reasonable. It includes prominences with names hallowed by official or historical usage. It has included some that are unfamiliar.

But land masses have a way of localizing themselves and stirring up controversy. Thus, if you wander the streets below Twin Peaks you will find neighborhoods firmly attached to a local bump with a local name.

You can take forty - two as the census of San Francisco hills, or you can deny it. The quarrel will never end.

And so we come to Irish Hill, the hill that isn't any more.

You could say it is down by the end of the horse car line, just across from the rolling mills. You could say it is 250 feet high, and

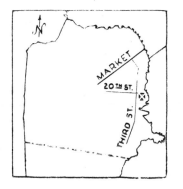

X marks Irish Hill.

ninety - eight wooden steps up from the corner of Twentieth and Illinois streets.

But you would be wrong in all save the location. What's left of it is still near the corner of Twentieth and Illinois, but there isn't much left.

Back in the 1880's and 1890's Irish Hill was indeed a hill, and lively, too. It was crowded with boarding houses and saloons. The Green House, the White House, Cash's, the Shasta House and Jim Gateley's San Quentin House were filled from one year to the next.

The boarding houses were home to thousands of young Irish immigrants who came to San Francisco to work in the mills and foundries that smoked along the shore of Potrero Point.

They worked twelve hours a day, and on Saturday nights they drank steam beer in Mike Boyes' Saloon on the very top of Irish Hill. They set up a rope ring in Mike's yard and crowned a new bare - knuckles champion every week.

Then in 1903 the great financier from the East, Charles M. Schwab, bought the Union Iron Works for a million dollars cash and turned it into part of the Bethlehem Steel empire.

In World War I the mills and Bethlehem yards grew swiftly; Irish Hill was doomed.

The boarding houses were razed, the buckos moved off to the Mission and the Potrero, and Irish Hill was attacked by shovels.

Part of the summit was leveled during that war as Bethlehem's plant took over.

In World War II, while ships poured out of Potrero Point, the hill was attacked again, and more was gouged away by bulldozers.

After the second war the hill was almost gone, but what was left raised a cloud of dust on every windy day. So the final indignity was heaped upon it. Workmen gunnited the slopes: they sprayed concrete on the hill's ruins, and left a remnant that looks almost like papier mache today, dwarfed by the Pacific Gas and

The view from Irish Hill: Bethlehem-Pacific Shipyards (right), Bethlehem offices (center), and the American Can Co. plant (left). The Bay Bridge can be seen in the dim distance.

Electric tanks that loom above it.

You can still climb a dirt path to the top of Old Irish Hill. It starts in the Bethlehem parking lot and winds less than fifty feet up. A few scraggly eucalyptus trees stand on the slope. Looking north from the summit you can see the Bay Bridge, hidden by the cranes and shops of the Bethlehem yards. Southward you can see the haze-bound Navy ships at Hunters Point. East is out across the Bay, and west brings into focus the frame houses on the back slopes of Potrero Hill.

And that is Irish Hill.

Nob Hill and Telegraph, Russian Hill and Mount Davidson have kept their lustre — and even added to it over the years.

But Irish Hill is derelict and forlorn, like a Mother Lode graveyard when the gold played out.

The city has passed it by.

What's left of Irish Hill is almost hidden by the shipyards and Potrero Point's gas tanks.

REFERENCE INDEX